SUGAR-FREE TODDLERS

SUGAR-FREE TODDLERS

Over 100 Recipes
Plus
Sugar Ratings For Store-bought Foods

SUSAN WATSON

Illustrations by Loretta Trezzo

WILLIAMSON PUBLISHING
CHARLOTTE, VERMONT 05445

Library of Congress Cataloging-in-Publication Data

Watson, Susan, 1964–
    Sugar–free toddlers: 125 sugarless recipes plus
sugar ratings for hundreds of storebought products /
Susan Watson.
        p. cm.
    Includes index
ISBN 0-913589-57-8 :
    1. Sugar–free diet—Recipes. 2. Children—Nutrition.
    I. Title.
RM237.85.W38 1991   91-19860
641.5'638—dc20   CPI

Cover and page design: Trezzo-Braren Studio
Illustrations: Loretta Trezzo
Printing: Capital City Press

Williamson Publishing Co.
Charlotte, Vermont 05445

Manufactured in the United States of America

10 9 8 7 6 5 4

Notice: The information contained in this book is true,
complete, and accurate to the best of our knowledge.
All recommendations and suggestions are made without
any guarantees on the part of the author or Williamson
Publishing. The author and publisher disclaim all liability
incurred in connection with the use of this information.

These recipes are not for diabetic children.

Contents

The Recipes

Sugar Ratings For Store–bought Foods

My first thanks must go to my husband Jim, who has given me unflagging support and encouragement throughout a year that has been unbelievably busy. Thanks also to my daughter (my number one test subject) for her inspiration. Special thanks go to my mother, who started me off so well with lots of love, and has always told me I could do whatever I set my mind to. Many thanks go to my wonderful friends and family for their constant encouragement: my grandparents; my brothers Jeff and David; all of my Watson and Knoblauch In-Laws; Pia and Warren Fay; the Georges; the Ryans; Steve Donnelly; Anne Shaffer; and Maureen, who helps cheer me up even in the worst moments. Finally, I want to thank Susan Williamson for all of her expert guidance and advice, and playing such an important role in getting a final product to be truly proud of.

Preface

Believe it or not, even the busiest, most harried parents can significantly reduce the amount of refined sugar their child eats. As a new mother several years ago, I wanted my daughter's transition to eating solid foods to be as healthy as possible. With both my husband and I working full time, we were concerned that time restraints might lead us to take the easy road instead of making the healthiest choices for our daughter. We weren't fanatical about health food, but we didn't want to simply feed her what seemed to be the most readily available baby and toddler foods, if we could find more nutritious alternatives.

I began to research the nutrition of young children. Much to my surprise, I discovered there is not much good information available—a paragraph here, a height and weight chart there, but little else except piecemeal data. With time and further research, I was able to compile a fairly comprehensive amount of nutritional information and product data relative to toddlers.

I quickly realized to what great extent brand name advertising had influenced our food buying patterns. And I quickly learned that we were not alone. Yet, not only are there many easy recipes for naturally sweetened foods that your child (yes!) will enjoy, but there is an ever-increasing number of naturally sweetened products that are prepackaged and ready to use, available in supermarkets and health food stores. These products include everything from toaster pastries and breakfast cereals to snack bars, cookies, and vitamins. A second conclusion I then came to was that feeding our daughter healthier yet still flavorful foods was easy! She loved these new foods!

Why bother?

Why should we reduce (or even eliminate) sugar from our children's diets? High concentrations of sugar greatly increase tooth decay, resulting in a high monetary cost as well as bodily deterioration. Refined sugar consumed over the course of a lifetime has been linked to heart disease, diabetes, stomach problems, hardening of the arteries, depression, and other serious illnesses. The Tide-water Detention Homes (a juvenile detention facility) in Tidewater, Virginia found that by significantly reducing just the amount of sugar in adolescents' diets, the rate of antisocial behavior dropped 44 percent. They also found that there were 82 percent fewer assault incidents, 77 percent fewer theft incidents, and 55 percent fewer incidents of refusal to obey requests!

Obesity in children has risen dramatically over the past fifty years, and this coincides directly with an increase in the use of refined sugars in prepared foods (many breakfast cereals have a sugar content of 30 percent or more). The typical person living in the United States consumes an average of 125 pounds of refined sugar per year. In order to eat the equivalent of eight ounces of refined sugar, a person would need to consume thirty-two apples. Clearly, our bodies were not intended to metabolize such high sugar concentrations.

But the most important reason for you to reduce or eliminate refined sugar in your child's diet is your child. We all want to give our children the healthiest diet possible, and a big part of this equation is sugar. Refined sugar adds empty calories to your child's body, not nutrients. In addition, it is considered anti-nutrient by nutritionists, because it actually robs vital minerals and B-vitamins as it is metabolized.

Using this book will help you gain control over the amount of refined sugar in your child's diet. This is not a fad diet book or a health food treatise. It is simply a guide to help you start your children off on the path toward healthier eating habits that we hope they will continue throughout their lives. Once you realize how much children like these sugar-free foods, you'll also realize how easy it is to start changing your own eating habits and those of your entire family. Although my husband and I did not plan to change our own eating habits, we have gradually eaten less and less sugar over the past several years. We enjoy many of the same foods that our daughter enjoys. And we truly feel better. We crave sugar much less frequently, and when we do indulge, it is a more controlled indulgence. I would never have believed it before, but now if I eat too much sugar, I feel queasy! It's as if my body is protesting this unnecessary invasion.

The nice thing about the following recipes and sugar-free products is that they allow your child to enjoy foods that are naturally sweetened and that taste and look just as good as the cookies his lunch neighbor is eating. This helps prevent feelings of being "weird" or "different." It's a great feeling as a parent to see your toddler munching on a nutrient-rich muffin that you baked yourself! Day-care and preschool teachers have frequently asked me what that wonderful aroma was emanating from my daughter's lunch box. It has been nice to be able to tell them it was a healthy, sugarless treat.

Although you may feel that you cannot completely eliminate refined sugar from your child's diet, the important thing is that you take control of the amount eaten. And, as my approach emphasizes convenience, you won't have to buy any expensive equipment or spend hours in the kitchen to get immediate results. Make a few small changes at first—perhaps being sure that midmorning and midafternoon snacks are sugar-free. You'll find it's a snap, and your wonderful child is well worth it!

TODDLERS & FOOD

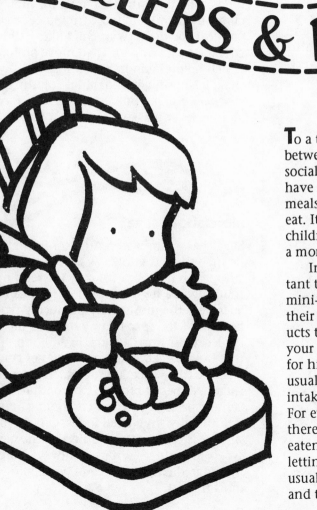

To a toddler, there is no real distinction made between a snack and a meal, except maybe the social interaction which accompanies each. Studies have shown that grazing, or eating many small meals, is the healthiest way for young children to eat. It leads to fewer weight problems, teaches children to trust their true appetites, and maintains a more consistent blood sugar level.

In light of this, it becomes even more important to provide children with snacks that are really mini-meals packed with nutrients to help meet their nutritional requirements. Recipes and products that are free of refined sugar allow you to give your child a greater variety of foods that are good for him and are fun to eat. This is because toddlers usually don't overeat, so the more of their caloric intake that is nutritious, the better off they'll be. For every empty sugar-laden calorie consumed, there is an equal reduction in nutritious calories eaten. Keeping sugar out of your child's diet means letting more of the good things in. Sugar-free usually means nutrient-rich, and that is what food and toddlers are all about.

Going sugar-free

Start as young as possible. The earlier you begin to introduce naturally-sweetened foods into your child's life, the more likely he or she is to readily accept them. Research has shown that children who eat low-sugar foods as babies do not develop as intense a sweet tooth. They do develop a greater appreciation for more healthful foods and eat them more enthusiastically. Studies have also demonstrated that babies who eat sugar at a very early age tend to develop a much stronger taste for sugar than those who were not exposed to it.

Be patient. Until age two, it is fairly easy to restrict the amount of sugar in your child's diet. Then, around age two, it becomes more difficult as your child is exposed to more and more social situations. However, your creativity and understanding can result in the successful limitation of sugar throughout childhood. Fortunately, also around age two, it becomes easier to explain exceptions and "special occasions." You know your child best, so follow your own good judgement when developing a framework for healthful eating.

Don't expect miracles. You can guide your child with patience, understanding, and care, but there will be times when he or she is out of your control. Explain to friends, relatives, and baby-sitters what your guidelines for sugar-free eating are, but don't be surprised when Grandma says, "No granddaughter of mine can go without a chocolate heart for Valentine's Day!"

Don't despair. If your child is older or already accustomed to traditionally sugared foods, introduce the new foods gradually, one at a time. Emphasize their taste, not their newness, and phase them in quietly, understanding that some will be liked more than others, as is true of all foods. First try those that are most similar to foods currently favored (choose fruit juice-sweetened oatmeal cookies, if your child likes oatmeal cookies, for example). Then move on to foods which might be more unfamiliar (like a yogurt shake). Not only is your child adjusting to the absence of sugar, but also to the new flavors that all that sugar masked, so go slowly.

More about sugar

Sugar has a number of often confusing forms. Refined sugar is known as *sucrose*, which is sugar stripped to its purest form by the refining process, resulting in a high calorie, low fiber carbohydrate. Sucrose is the most cavity-producing type of sugar because of the specific way that it is metabolized by decay-causing bacteria. In addition, the bond that holds together the molecules of glucose and fructose (that make up sucrose) happens to make sucrose a special promoter of tooth decay. Sucrose is the type of sugar most commonly found in traditionally sweetened foods. On ingredient lists, sucrose is called sugar, confectioners' sugar, corn syrup, and other "syrups." (Always remember that ingredients are listed in descending order—most to least.)

Glucose is known as blood sugar because it is always present in our bloodstream. It is necessary for the functioning of the brain and nervous system and is a key ingredient in our metabolism of plant and animal matter. Glucose is usually found with other sugars in fruits and vegetables.

Lactose is the sugar found naturally in milk. *Fructose* is the sugar found naturally in fruits. It is easier to digest than sucrose because it does not need insulin in order to get into the liver and other cells, as sucrose does. Fructose is 70 percent sweeter than sucrose, and thus it takes fewer calories to achieve the same sweetness. This makes it a healthier alternative when it is consumed at the levels in which it naturally occurs, but not as a highly concentrated "artificial" sweetener.

What about carbohydrates?

Complex carbohydrates are the starches (grain products and vegetables) and naturally occurring sugars (glucose/fructose in fruits and plants, lactose in milk). Complex carbohydrates are metabolized by the body over time, allowing a slow, even release of energy. In addition, foods that contain complex carbohydrates in their natural, unrefined form (grains, fruit, and milk) also contain vitamins, minerals, and fiber needed by the human body. Soluble fiber like *pectin*, found in apples and citrus fruits, helps to slow glucose absorption by the body.

Simple carbohydrates are the simple sugars, such as sucrose and fructose. *They provide only calories —no nutrients.* They are found naturally, in very small amounts, in fruits and vegetables. However, it is in their refined and processed form that we find the bulk of simple sugars in the typical diet. And you'll be surprised where it shows up. I was shocked to discover that the cranberry juice I had come to love had, in fact, 50 percent of its calories attributable to added sucrose! And I thought I was drinking a healthy juice!

Simple sugars are also found in concentrated amounts in such supposedly healthy sweeteners as honey, molasses, brown sugar, and maple syrup. Don't be fooled by the huge array of products out there that call themselves "healthy" and "natural" just because they happen to contain honey. *Honey is a highly concentrated simple sugar, only minutely and insignificantly better for you than table sugar.*

Although simple sugars are immediate energy sources, they are too quickly metabolized (usually in thirty minutes) to give any real energy benefits. They cause a rapid rise in blood sugar levels that overstimulates the secretion of insulin. This causes a longer-term lowering of blood sugar levels, robbing the brain and nervous system of the glucose they need to function.

Honey, molasses, brown sugar, & maple syrup

Although these simple sugars are considered by many people to be "less refined," they are highly concentrated forms of simple sugars (close to 100 percent sugar), and as such will not be included as sweeteners in this book. For example, honey is 75 percent sucrose and 25 percent fructose. Although honey does contain some of the nutrients phosphorus, potassium, and calcium, the amounts are so minute that a person would need to consume more than sixteen cups of honey per day in order to fulfill her daily phosphorus requirements, more than five cups for potassium, and more than twelve cups for calcium! One cup of honey has about 990 calories, a cup of sucrose (table sugar) has about 750 calories. A study at Oregon State University demonstrated that some honeys may carry carcinogens in the substances bees have extracted from the flowers. Additionally, honey should not be served to children under one year because it may contain spores of the bacterium *Clostridium botulinum*, which is harmless to adults but can cause botulism in infants.

Molasses is the liquid refined from sugar cane or beet juice, after the crystals of sucrose have been removed. It contains several simple sugars, as well as water and a few nutrients at levels that may be considered significant. Since it is a refined form of concentrated sugars, I don't consider it a healthy or necessary alternative for children.

Maple syrup is simply concentrated liquid sugar from maple trees. Brown sugar is table sugar (sucrose) with a bit of molasses added for color and flavor. Neither has any significant nutritional value other than calories.

Artificial sweeteners

The aim of this book is to provide healthy, convenient alternatives for feeding your child. The foods recommended here are not necessarily low in calories, because this is not intended as a weight-loss program for children. Any of these recipes or products should be incorporated into a program of balanced, nutritious meals and snacks for your family. As with everything, moderation is the key.

Artificial sweeteners (saccharine, aspartame, and others) have been variously linked to health problems. Although some of these findings are disputable, it is always best to take the safe route for your child. More importantly, these artificial sweeteners are not needed in a healthy diet. Wouldn't you prefer for your child to eat a muffin sweetened with apple juice instead of saccharine? Also, artificial sweeteners provide only sweetness. Like refined sugar, they offer no nutrients and do not belong in most young children's diets.

Nutritional meal planning

Knowing the nutritional requirements of a typical toddler will help you incorporate the recipes and products presented here into your toddler's diet. Government standards for toddler requirements of each nutrient are listed, as well as examples of servings that meet these needs. *A toddler serving size for these purposes equals approximately half an adult portion.* Since every child is unique, please consult with your pediatrician for specific guidelines for your child.

There is no such thing as a typical toddler meal. Add, mix and match, and don't limit a meal to its "traditional" foods. There's nothing wrong with grilled cheese for breakfast or eggs for dinner! Always emphasize variety and creativity to keep toddlers interested. Here's an example of how a day's meals and snacks can satisfy nutritional needs:

Breakfast: 1 egg with 1 ounce cheese melted in, 4 orange sections, 1 cup whole milk

Snack: 1/2 cup orange juice, 3 whole grain crackers with peanut butter

Lunch: ham and cheese on whole grain bread, 1 cup milk, 2 tablespoons raisins, whole grain fruit cookie

Snack: 1 cup water, carrot stick, hard cheese slice

Dinner: 1 cup milk, 2 ounces chicken breast meat, whole grain roll with butter, broccoli

Snack: 1/2 banana, whole milk yogurt with fruit blended in

You may find, as I did, that your child has no desire to touch (let alone eat) some of the foods that you know are nutrient rich. I'm all too familiar with the "I–don't–like–this" dilemma! Try to make a fair analysis of which requirements are being met. Then discuss it with your pediatrician to see whether or not a vitamin supplement is recommended.

Some foods satisfy more than one requirement, so keep this in mind when planning your child's meals. Broccoli, for example, satisfies calcium, green vegetable, and vitamin C requirements.

Toddler nutritional requirements

Calories: *average 900 - 1350 per day* (depending on size and activity level). If your toddler's weight at check-up time is staying on a continual curve, he or she is probably getting the right amount of calories. Be sure to allow for the dips and curves of normal growth spurts.

Protein: *4 servings.* One serving = $3/4$ cup milk; $1/2$ cup yogurt; $3/4$ ounce hard cheese; 1 whole egg or 2 egg whites; 1 ounce fish, poultry, or meat; $1 1/2$ tablespoons peanut butter; or 1 ounce pasta

Vitamin C: *2 to 4 servings.* One serving = $1/2$ orange; $1/8$ cantaloupe; $1/4$ grapefruit; $1/4$ cup citrus juice; $1/4$ cup broccoli; 1 small tomato; $1/2$ cup tomato juice; or $1/4$ green pepper

Calcium: *4 servings.* One serving = $2/3$ cup milk; $1/4$ cup nonfat dry milk; $1/2$ cup yogurt; 1 ounce hard cheese; $1/2$ cup calcium fortified citrus juice; 1 cup cooked broccoli; 1 cup greens; or 2 ounces canned salmon with bones crushed in

Green leafy and yellow vegetables/yellow fruits: *2 to 3 servings.* One serving = 1 apricot; $1/2$ cup cantaloupe; 1 nectarine; $1/2$ cup cooked broccoli; 6 asparagus spears; $1/2$ cup peas; $1/2$ carrot; 1 tablespoon sweet potato; 1 small tomato; $1/4$ red bell pepper; $3/4$ cup tomato juice

Other fruits and vegetables: *2 servings.* One serving = $1/2$ apple; $1/2$ pear; 1 plum; 1 small banana; $1/4$ cup unsweetened applesauce; 1 fig; $1/2$ slice pineapple; 2 tablespoons raisins; $1/4$ cup squash; $1/4$ avocado; $1/3$ cup peas; or $1/2$ ear of corn

Complex carbohydrates: *4 to 5 servings.* One serving = 1 tablespoon wheat germ; $1/2$ slice whole grain bread; $1/4$ whole wheat bagel; $1/4$ cup brown or wild rice; $1/2$ cup of whole grain breakfast cereal

Iron: *At least one iron-rich food per day.* These include beef, soy flour, dried fruit, spinach, tuna, sunflower seeds, scallops, clams, and carob. Vitamin C eaten with iron aids in the absorption of iron by the body.

Fat: *6 to 7 servings.* One serving = 1 tablespoon peanut butter; 1 egg; $1/2$ teaspoon margarine; $3/4$ cup whole milk yogurt; 2 tablespoons sour cream; $2/3$ ounce hard cheese. Toddlers should get about 30 percent of their daily calories from fat. Sufficient fat is needed to support growth, brain development, and motor coordination, so a healthy amount of fat must be included in toddlers' diets. After age two, doctors recommend a slight cutting back on fat, by doing such things as using 2-percent milk instead of whole milk. But even children older than two should not be on severe, fat restricted diets. Check with your pediatrician for specific guidelines for your child. Discuss with him or her recommendations about fat intake and cholesterol levels, given the new data being made available concerning recommended levels for young children.

Fluids: *4 to 6 cups additional to the fluids found in foods.* One cup milk = $2/3$ fluid serving. Fruit and vegetable juices and water are the healthiest fluids.

Brown Bag Lunches

Even when we can't be with them, we want our children to eat nutritious foods. The problem is that when children are at school, we aren't there to help make the meal enticing and interesting. What can be done to prevent your child from ignoring or tossing out the lunch and snack you packed?

You can succeed in packing taste, nutrition, and convenience! One of the keys is to emphasize variety. Keep a varied supply of healthy whole grain breads, cheeses, fruits, vegetables, and meats in your refrigerator and freezer to give your child a good variety of meals. Moving toward more variety is healthier as well as being more interesting to your child. Variety also helps many children remain receptive to trying new foods as they get older.

Most children of any age love to find a surprise in their lunch! Try putting a funny sticker, a photo, picture, or even just a happy face in toddler lunches to help perk up their interest. Older children enjoy a simple note reminding them that you are thinking about them. Simple is best; you don't want the note to distract from the lunch, but to enhance it!

Vegetables. Keep plenty of fresh vegetables pre-prepared in your refrigerator.Carrot sticks will store well in a container of water in your refrigerator. Cut-up broccoli florets will store well in an airtight bag for about two weeks. Keep a clean cucumber on hand, and slice off a thick piece as a lunch box supplement. Teethers in particular like to chew on a nice cold piece of cucumber, especially in the summer. I call it Toddler Watermelon!

Cheese. Vary not only the kind of cheese but also the form to keep interest high. Use spreads on cracker "sandwiches," provide string cheese sticks which toddlers seem to love, send small cups or baggies of grated cheese, pack wrapped slices of American cheese or small squares of mild cheddar, or spread cream cheese on a whole grain bagel.

Meats. Dice up toddler-safe sized chunks of low-sodium ham. Store them in an airtight container in the freezer, and simply pour a portion as you need it into a sealable container to send in lunches. It will thaw safely by lunch time. Roll up meat and bologna slices with or without cheese in the middle. Send a roll or two to school in a baggy. Toss tuna with grated cheese and carrot for an inviting, colorful treat.

Fruits. Send fresh whole fruit to be peeled or cut up by a teacher, if your child isn't old enough. Individual sealed cups of unsweetened applesauce are readily available in grocery stores, or prepare your own. Individual servings (packets or small boxes) of raisins and/or dried fruit make a welcome, nutritious shack. Cut up a variety of fresh fruits and send mixed fruit cups in sealable containers. These are also available in pre-pack cans in grocery stores, but many have added sugar, so read the labels carefully.

Breads. Try whole grain low-salt crackers, plain or spread with cheese or peanut butter. Most bagels, English muffins, and pita bread are now available in whole grain form. Send a whole grain muffin. Vary the type of grain in the bread often, if your child likes several kinds. Many toddlers prefer oatmeal bread.

Hints for packaging day-care lunches

Packing day-care lunches is different from packing regular school lunches, and what is appropriate also varies from center to center. There is normally refrigeration available for storing food items, and the parent may transport the lunch box yielding minimum tossing about. This gives you much greater flexibility in choosing your toddler's menu.

There is great variation from center to center as to how meals are presented and how much supervision is provided. Is your child given his or her lunch to eat or pick at as he or she pleases, or is it "served" to the child with supervision? "Not eating your sandwich, Peter? Okay, let's try some carrot sticks! Ummm, these look good. Here you go." Hopefully, at least younger children are given guidance, supervision, and encouragement. Snack time also varies from center to center. Will you need to supply snacks or does the center or day-care provider supply them? Typically, parents supply at least one of the snacks, but you may want to provide more than that if you don't like the center's snack menu. Remember: to a toddler a snack is pretty much the same as a meal, so don't waste the opportunity to provide nutrition plus a treat.

When packing the lunch and snacks, it is best to separate the items needing refrigeration from those that do not. This maintains better quality, by allowing the crackers to stay crisp, as well as the carrots. Toddlers know the difference; nobody likes a soggy cracker! Use airtight containers as much as possible to maintain quality and freshness. There are a great variety of sealable plastic containers on the market that work very well. And they're toddler crushproof! Buy the smallest containers you can find for very young children. They are made round, square, and rectangular, so choose those that fit your lunch boxes and menus best. Zip-loc type baggies work well also, but are not reusable.

For school lunches without refrigeration, take advantage of the small ice packs now available that fit into lunch boxes. There are even flexible ice "wraps" that you can sandwich items in between to keep them cold. Try to use non-spoiling and frozen items as much as possible, allowing them to thaw during the morning classes so that they are ready to eat at lunch. For an informative look at packing school lunches, I refer you to *The Brown Bag Cookbook* by Sara Sloan (Williamson Publishing Co.).

Chapter 2

HEALTHY & DELICIOUS

The recipes that follow were designed primarily to accomplish three things: to be sugar-free and as nutritious as possible, to appeal to toddlers' tastes, and to be as convenient as possible for you to prepare and use. I have tried to balance these three considerations as much as possible. After all, it is counterproductive for foods to be nutritious, if toddlers won't eat them; it is useless for foods to be flavorful and nutritious, if they are too complex or time-consuming to prepare; and it defeats the purpose if foods taste good but contain only empty calories. We have plenty of those recipes in everyday cookbooks! I have included just a few special recipes that are somewhat more time-consuming (for example, the Pineapple-Coconut Custard) for those special occasions when you are able to put in extra time and effort.

The recipes incorporate ingredients that are as nutritious as possible without being hard to find. Salt has been added only in a few cases, where the flavor, texture, or freshness of the product demands it. You will probably find that you already have many of the ingredients on hand, but some may be new to your cooking routine. Most are commonly found in grocery stores (often in the diet foods section or the health foods section). Depending on where you live, you might need to buy a few of the ingredients in health food stores or co-ops.

Common ingredients

Low-sodium baking powder

Since the sodium amounts in a toddler's regular meals are sufficient to fulfill his or her daily requirements, low-sodium baking powder is recommended for recipes. It is generally used at 1 1/2 times the amount of regular baking powder, so *adjust the level accordingly, if you use regular baking powder* in these recipes. (If a recipe calls for 3 teaspoons low-sodium, use 2 teaspoons of the regular.) If your grocery store does not carry low-sodium baking powder, ask them to order it or check with local health food stores about its availability. One common brand is Featherweight, manufactured by Sandoz Nutrition, Minneapolis, Minnesota 55416.

Whole wheat flour

With many more nutrients than bleached white flour (the bleaching process removes about sixteen nutrients from the flour), whole grain flour is the preferred flour in many recipes. It is rich in B-vitamins and protein. Whole wheat flour is readily available in most grocery stores. Stone-ground whole grain flour is preferred because stone grinding is less destructive to the vitamins in the grain than steel grinding, which uses much more heat. Whole grain flours tend to spoil much more quickly than white flour, so storage in the refrigerator is recommended.

Other flours

Unbleached white flour is used in recipes in which whole wheat flour has proven to be too heavy to produce good flavor and texture. It is now commonly found in grocery stores and is more nutritious than its bleached counterpart. Again, whenever possible, use the stone-ground variety.

Stone-ground corn meal is readily available in many stores and is also a more nutritious choice than bleached white flour. It provides a nice, crumbly texture and a naturally sweet taste to many foods.

Barley, oat, rice, and soy flours can easily be added in small amounts (25 percent) in most recipes calling for wheat flour, without concern. Because of their varying amounts of gluten, these flours should not be used as 100 percent substitutions in most recipes, but they are nice additions to the flavor of whole wheat and unbleached white flour recipes. Soy flour has no gluten, but it is rich in protein, B-vitamins and vitamin E, and lecithin. The lecithin and vitamin E act as natural preservatives in baked products.

Frozen juice concentrates

The most commonly used types are apple juice and white grape juice concentrates. They are easy to keep on hand and are readily available. The amount needed for a recipe can be scooped out and thawed, and the remainder covered and returned to the freezer for later use. Be sure to check the list of ingredients on each brand to make sure that no sugars have been added. Some brands which advertise "all natural" on their labels still contain added sugar.

Unsweetened fruit juices and unsweetened applesauce

Again, check the label for a list of ingredients. Manufacturers are making it more and more difficult to determine at a glance whether a product contains added sugar. Many are now calling sucrose a natural sweetener on their products, further complicating the issue.

Peanut butter

Natural peanut butter is now readily available in most grocery stores. Some even have it freshly made on the premises with nothing added. Check the label! Peanut butter provides flavor that most toddlers love, and contains a healthy amount of protein and, for those under two, fat. Try grinding your own, too.

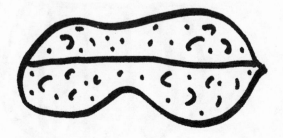

Wheat germ

It is readily available in its toasted form, which is still extremely nutritious. Three tablespoons contain 30 percent of the U.S. RDA for a child of protein, 60 percent of thiamine, 20 percent of riboflavin, 20 percent of iron, 60 percent of vitamin E, 16 percent of vitamin B6, 50 percent of folic acid, 60 percent of phosphorus, 40 percent of magnesium, 60 percent of zinc, and 8 percent of copper, as well as 6 grams of complex carbohydrates, 3 grams of simple carbohydrates (nothing's perfect) and 3 grams of dietary fiber! Wheat germ can easily be added to most recipes for great nutritional impact. For even more nutritional impact, it is sometimes available in health food stores untoasted, preserving more nutrients. Store all wheat germ in the refrigerator for maximum freshness.

Fresh fruit

Nutrient and fiber rich, fresh fruit is delicious on its own and a healthful addition to many recipes.

Canned fruit

Canned fruit is a convenient alternative to fresh fruit, especially when your favorite fruit is not in season. Be sure to get the type that is packed in its own juices, and not the heavy or light syrup varieties which contain added sugar.

Dried fruit

Invaluable to the taste of many baked goods, dried fruit is rich in iron and fiber and lends itself well to enhancing the flavor of many recipes. Raisins, dates, and figs are frequently used to give a natural sweetness to recipes. By chopping them in a blender or food processor, you make them safe for all toddlers (and almost invisible to finicky eaters). Dates and figs are often packaged as sugared, so be careful to buy the unsugared varieties. Dried pears, apples, and apricots are becoming more readily available (they are often in bins in the store's bulk foods section) and are also nutritious, flavorful additions. If possible, try to buy dried fruit which is unsulphured, that is, without added sulphur products as preservatives.

Vegetable cooking spray

This quickly becomes a convenient addition to your kitchen baking artillery. It is quick, easy, and healthful, and keeps your baked goods from becoming unwanted additions to your baking pan!

Nonfat dry milk powder

Inexpensive and easy to use, this powder is rich in calcium. It retains the calcium potency of regular milk as well as the protein. One-third cup of dry milk equals a full protein serving. It can easily be added to breakfast cereals, batters, and milk beverages to boost your toddler's calcium and protein intake.

Carob

Carob is available in the form of flour, powder, and chips in most health food stores. It substitutes well for cocoa and chocolate, without the caffeine or sugar. It is also a fairly good source of iron.

Kitchen tools

Beyond the usual baking utensils (measuring cups and spoons, mixing bowls, cookie sheets, muffin pans), you will need either a blender or food processor to chop or mix ingredients in many of these recipes. I have specified a blender because it seems to be more common to most households and is easy to use and clean. If you have a food processor, you can easily use it with any of these recipes. Blenders and food processors are invaluable in chopping fruit and nuts into toddler-safe bits.

Nutritional quotients

Included for each recipe is what I call the nutritional quotient for one serving of each recipe. The nutritional quotient is an approximate listing of the toddler's daily nutritional requirements that are fulfilled by that one serving. So if the recipe indicates that the "Nutritional quotient = 1 protein, 1 whole grain," it means that one serving of that recipe fulfills a toddler's daily nutritional requirement for one serving of protein and one serving of a whole grain food. These daily requirements are listed on page 16. All nutritional quotients are estimates based on ingredients and serving size and should be incorporated into a regular nutritional plan for your child. Since each child is slightly different, please consult your pediatrician for more specific guidelines.

Toddler ratings

Each recipe and sugar-free product has been taste-tested by a series of babies and toddlers. The children of friends and day-care acquaintances, as well as children at nearby day-care centers were my willing subjects in an ongoing eat-a-thon. Feedback from teachers and parents, as well as my own observations and discussions with the toddlers, were used to arrive at an overall toddler rating for each recipe or product. Recipes that rated less than an 8 out of 10 were deemed unsatisfactory and are not included. All prepackaged products are included in store–bought evaluations regardless of their rating. I did not, however, have the children taste test the sugared items. By having the toddlers rate the products and recipes, I hope to have dramatically increased your success rate!

Preparation time

There have been many times when I started to make a recipe, only to find out halfway through that it was going to take twice the amount of time I allotted! To help you plan your time, I have included a basic, easy-to-read preparation time near the top of each recipe. In arriving at the preparation time, I included time to gather the ingredients and work through the recipe. I have tried to make that figure as realistic as possible, but I didn't include any time for interruptions, so keep that in mind!

Making it easy on yourself

You might be asking yourself, "How in the world can I find the time to bake a batch of muffins?" There are always those weekends when you find yourself going in ten different directions. I, too, am constantly juggling to get everything done (which never happens), but I have managed, once a month, to put aside the time to bake a few batches of snacks to use throughout the following month in my daughter's snacks and lunches. It only takes about an hour to make enough for a month. I freeze the snacks in individual serving-sized bags or wrap. Throughout the month, I actually save time because the snacks are prepared and ready to go.

Freezing tips

Nearly all of the baked goods presented here will freeze extremely well, with the exception of biscuits, which tend to dry out quickly. Unfortunately, the toppings and most sauces do not do well in the freezer, but do remain fresh in the refrigerator for up to ten days when sealed in an airtight container. Pancakes and griddle pies freeze fairly well, and all of the crackers can be frozen, although they become very breakable and must be handled carefully.

For baked goods: Allow to cool completely. This minimizes the amount of condensate which freezes in the container with the baked goods. Wrap each piece individually, in wrap or a baggy. Then seal the pieces into an airtight freezer container. Large zip-loc type freezer bags work well for some items, and they can be rinsed out and reused. With others, medium-sized square or round plastic freezer containers protect the items from being squashed. It is important to have this

double layer of protection for two reasons: It keeps the foods from drying out in today's frost-free freezers (which take the moisture out of everything in the freezer) and double-wrapping makes it very convenient to grab one piece for a lunch or snack and put it directly into a lunch box or microwave to thaw. Most of these wraps can be reused.

For pancakes and griddle pies: Allow to cool completely. Seal several at a time into airtight freezer bags. To reheat, see microwave guidelines. A great way to save leftovers or have breakfast ready to go in minutes!

For crackers: Allow to cool completely. Seal in small batches in airtight freezer bags. Then seal the bags into a crush-proof freezer container. Thaw at room temperature only, to prevent crumbling.

Allow foods to thaw at room temperature. This usually takes from one to two hours. A cookie or muffin which is put into a lunch box frozen will have thawed perfectly by lunch time (and keeps the other foods chilled, too). To thaw in the microwave, wrap in a paper towel and thaw just to room temperature or a bit warmer. This keeps the baked good moist and allows the natural flavors of the ingredients to come out.

Every microwave is different, so experiment to see what works best for thawing baked goods for you. It is better to under thaw, rather than to risk starting to cook them again. If you have a defrost setting on your microwave, use that. Here are some general microwave times to thaw frozen baked goods (just to about room temperature):

muffins	15-20 seconds on reheat or high
quick bread sticks	10-12 seconds on reheat or high
quick bread slices	15-20 seconds on reheat or high
cookies	10-12 seconds on reheat or high

Pancakes and griddle pies warm up nicely in the microwave. Place the desired number on a microwave safe plate. For each pancake or griddle pie, allow about 10 seconds on reheat or high. This will make them steamy enough to melt margarine.

So now, let's feed those hungry children some great tasting, good-for-them foods. Let's get cookin'!

The Recipes

Chapter 3

MAIN DISHES WITH TODDLER APPEAL

From breakfast to lunch to supper time, these recipes provide hearty, healthful main courses (and a few side dishes) for toddlers to enjoy. Many recipes also work well for babies who are eating solid foods (see *Make-Your-Own Baby Granola, Corny Spoon Bread,* and others), and most of the recipes please older children and parents, as well!

Keep in mind the adage "Variety is the spice of life" in planning toddler meals. Toddlers enjoy a variety in their menus like we all do, but they have no preconceived notions as to which foods belong at which meals. Thus, most love to eat *William Tell Pancakes* for dinner, and they don't think twice about having an *Aztec Power Breakfast* turned into a power lunch! Keeping children interested in healthful meals is one of the biggest food challenges parents have (as you know) and giving them new menu combinations is a great way to start making meals fun.

HIDDEN SECRET PANCAKES

TODDLER RATING: 8 out of 10

PREP TIME: 10–12 minutes

NUTRITIONAL QUOTIENT IN TWO 4-INCH PANCAKES = $1/2$ whole grain, $1/2$ green vegetable, $1/2$ protein, some calcium

Makes twelve 4-inch pancakes

These pancakes are so deliciously spiced, kids don't even realize that they are packed with vitamin A-rich zucchini!

1	cup whole milk
$1/4$	cup apple juice concentrate, thawed
2	tablespoons vegetable oil or melted margarine
2	eggs
$3/4$	cup whole wheat flour
$3/4$	cup unbleached white flour
$1/2$	cup wheat germ
$2^1/2$	teaspoons low-sodium baking powder
$1^1/2$	teaspoons vanilla extract
$1/2$	teaspoon nutmeg
1	cup grated zucchini, dried with paper towels

In a mixing bowl, combine the whole milk, juice, oil or margarine, and eggs. Mix thoroughly, then add remaining ingredients except the zucchini, and beat just until smooth. Fold in the zucchini. Coat a griddle with vegetable spray; heat to medium high. Reduce heat to medium and spoon on batter to make 4-inch pancakes. Heat until the surface bubbles and the bottoms are golden brown. Flip and brown the other side. Cool slightly before serving. Top with any of the sauces or syrups listed in toppings chapter.

AZTEC POWER BREAKFAST

TODDLER RATING: 8 out of 10

PREP TIME: 10–12 minutes

NUTRITIONAL QUOTIENT IN $2/3$ CUP = 1 whole grain, 1 protein, 1 calcium, some iron

Makes about 2 cups

*A calcium-rich hot breakfast cereal with the naturally sweet cornmeal flavor that most children love. Great topped with **Sweet Raisin Sauce**.*

$1/2$	cup whole grain yellow cornmeal
2	cups water
$2/3$	cup nonfat dry milk powder
$1/2$	cup whole milk yogurt
$1/4$	cup wheat germ
$3/4$	cup cottage cheese
$2/3$	cup raisins

Mix $1/2$ cup of the water with the raisins and put in a blender jar. Blend on medium until the raisins are completely chopped. In a mixing bowl, combine the water and raisin mixture with the cornmeal. Mix until smooth. Put the remaining $1^1/2$ cups of water into a saucepan and bring to a boil. Add the cornmeal mixture to the boiling water and stir until the mixture comes to a boil again. Reduce the heat to low and simmer 6 minutes, stirring frequently. Add the dry milk, yogurt, and wheat germ, and stir until hot. Stir in the cottage cheese. Cool slightly before serving in a small bowl.

GRIDDLE PUMPKIN PIES

TODDLER EATING: 9 out of 10

PREP TIME: 12 minutes

NUTRITIONAL QUOTIENT IN 2 PIES =
1 yellow vegetable, $^1/_2$ protein,
some whole grain

Makes about eight 2-inch pies

Two large, cooked sweet potatoes can be substituted for the pumpkin in this recipe. Great topped with yogurt or apple butter!

$1^1/_4$ cups packed canned pumpkin (unsweetened)
$^1/_2$ cup milk
2   eggs
$^1/_2$ cup whole wheat flour
1   teaspoon lemon juice
     Vegetable oil for frying

Combine all of the ingredients except the oil in a large mixing bowl. Mix thoroughly. Form into 2-inch patties about $^1/_4$ inch thick (no thicker than that or they will not cook properly). Heat 2 tablespoons of oil in a frying pan on medium heat. Saute the patties about 3 minutes on each side until golden brown. Drain on a paper towel and cool slightly before serving. Two large cooked sweet potatoes can be substituted for the pumpkin in this recipe.

BREAKFAST SHAKE

TODDLER RATING: 9 out of 10
PREP TIME: 5 minutes
NUTRITIONAL QUOTIENT IN 1 CUP =
1 calcium, 1 fruit, vitamin C,
some protein

Makes 1 cup

Who says breakfast can't be fun? Try this cooling shake on a hot summer's morn!

$^1/_2$ cup orange juice
$^1/_2$ cup nonfat dry milk powder
$^1/_2$ fresh banana
1 tablespoon wheat germ
$^1/_4$ cup plain yogurt

Combine all ingredients in a blender jar and mix on medium until the desired consistency is reached. Serve with banana slices or other fresh fruit.

WILLIAM TELL PANCAKES

TODDLER RATING: 10 out of 10
PREP TIME: 10–12 minutes
NUTRITIONAL QUOTIENT IN TWO 4-INCH PANCAKES = $^1/_2$ whole grain, some protein, some calcium, some fruit

Makes about twelve 4-inch pancakes

*These apple-flavored pancakes have an almost universal appeal to children of all ages. For a special treat, serve with warm **Garden of Eden Syrup**.*

$^1/_2$ cup whole wheat flour
$^1/_2$ cup unbleached white flour
3 teaspoons low-sodium baking powder
1 egg
1 cup whole milk
2 tablespoons vegetable oil or melted margarine
2 tablespoons apple juice concentrate, thawed
$^1/_2$ cup applesauce

Combine all ingredients in a mixing bowl and mix until smooth. Coat a griddle with vegetable spray; heat to medium high. Reduce heat to medium, then spoon on batter to make 4-inch pancakes. Heat until the surface bubbles and the bottoms are golden brown. Then flip and brown the remaining side. Cool slightly before serving. Try topped with *Homemade No-Cook Applesauce*, too.

APPLE FRITTERS

TODDLER RATING: 10 out of 10
PREP TIME: 12–15 minutes
NUTRITIONAL QUOTIENT IN ONE
FRITTER = some calcium, some
protein, some fruit

Makes about 15 fritters

These easy donuts are guaranteed winners with the entire family!

1   cup unbleached white flour
1³/₄ teaspoons low-sodium baking powder
¹/₂ teaspoon nutmeg
2   eggs
¹/₃ cup milk
2   tablespoons apple juice concentrate
1   teaspoon vegetable oil
¹/₂ cup diced apple bits
Oil for frying

Combine dry ingredients; mix and set aside. Beat together the eggs, milk, juice concentrate, and teaspoon vegetable oil. Stir in dry ingredients mixture. Fold in apple bits. In hot oil, drop batter by the teaspoonful and fry until golden brown. Drain on paper towels and cool to safe temperature before serving to your toddler.

HOT & FRUITY OATMEAL

TODDLER RATING: 8 out of 10
PREP TIME: 12 minutes
NUTRITIONAL QUOTIENT IN ¹/₂ CUP =
1 whole grain, 1 calcium, ¹/₂ fruit,
¹/₂ protein

Makes about 2 cups

*By getting the ingredients together the night before, you can make this deliciously fruity oatmeal a convenience even on a busy morning. Great with **Pick-Your-Flavor Jam Sauce!***

1¹/₂ cups water
¹/₄ cup apple juice concentrate, thawed
²/₃ cup rolled oats (not the quick kind)
²/₃ cup diced fresh or canned fruit, or 1/4 cup dried fruit
²/₃ cup nonfat dry milk powder
¹/₃ cup wheat germ
A pinch of cinnamon

In a saucepan, combine the water and apple juice concentrate, and bring to a boil. Reduce heat to low, then add the oats and cover. Simmer for 5 minutes. Add the fruit and cook for five more minutes. Add the milk powder, wheat germ, and cinnamon. Stir until the milk powder is dissolved and the ingredients are well combined. Cool to a safe temperature and serve in a small bowl. Top with milk if desired.

CORNY SPOON BREAD

TODDLER RATING: 10 out of 10
PREP TIME: 10 minutes, plus 1 hour to bake
NUTRITIONAL QUOTIENT IN 1 SERVING = 1 calcium, $^3/_4$ protein, some whole grain

Makes about 8 toddler servings

A delicious and nutritious brunch for your toddler, this spoon bread will keep for up to one week in the refrigerator.

3 cups whole milk
1¼ cups whole grain yellow cornmeal
1½ teaspoons low-sodium baking powder
2 tablespoons apple juice concentrate, thawed
2 tablespoons vegetable oil
3 eggs, separated

Preheat the oven to 350°. In a saucepan, heat 2 cups of the milk over medium heat, until it begins to simmer. Add the cornmeal. Continue to cook, stirring frequently, until the mixture thickens. Remove it from the heat and add the baking powder, juice concentrate, oil, and remaining milk. Beat the egg yolks slightly, and then add them to the cornmeal mixture. Beat the egg whites until stiff; fold them into the cornmeal mixture. Spray a 2-quart baking dish with vegetable cooking spray. Turn the mixture into it. Bake for about 1 hour, until brown on top. Serve topped with margarine in a small bowl for your toddler.

NUTRI CAKE

TODDLER RATING: 10 out of 10
PREP TIME: 10 minutes plus 25 minutes to bake
NUTRITIONAL QUOTIENT IN 1 SERVING = 1 fruit, 1 iron, $^3/_4$ whole grain, $^1/_2$ protein

Makes 10 servings

Here's a cake nutritional enough to qualify as breakfast!

1	medium banana, mashed
$^1/_2$	cup soft margarine
3	eggs
1	teaspoon vanilla extract
$1^1/_2$	cups whole wheat flour
$1^1/_2$	cups unbleached white flour
$^1/_4$	cup wheat germ
$1^1/_2$	cups water
1	teaspoon baking soda
3	teaspoons low-sodium baking powder
$1^1/_2$	cups chopped dates

Preheat oven to 350°. Cream together the margarine and the banana. Add eggs, vanilla, and water and mix thoroughly. Add dry ingredients except the dates and mix well. Fold in chopped dates. Pour batter into a greased and floured 9 x 13 baking pan and spread evenly. Bake for 20–25 minutes until an inserted toothpick comes out clean. Cool before serving.

ASK-FOR-MORE CHEESY GRIDDLE CAKES

TODDLER RATING: 9 out of 10
PREP TIME: 10–12 minutes
NUTRITIONAL QUOTIENT IN TWO 4-INCH PANCAKES = 1 calcium, some protein

Makes about eight 4-inch pancakes

These taste great alone or with jam toppings, and make an excellent and satisfying lunch.

1   cup unbleached white flour
3   teaspoons low-sodium baking powder
1   egg
1¼ cups whole milk
2   tablespoons wheat germ
2   tablespoons vegetable oil
⅔ cup grated cheese
    (cheddar and mozzarella combined work nicely)

In a mixing bowl, combine all ingredients except the cheese. Mix thoroughly until smooth; fold in the grated cheese. Coat a griddle with vegetable spray; heat to medium high. Drop batter by the spoonful to make 4-inch pancakes. Heat until the surface bubbles and the bottoms are golden brown. Flip and heat the other side until it is also golden brown. Cool slightly before serving.

MAKE-YOUR-OWN BABY GRANOLA

BABY RATING: Babies seem to enjoy eating this granola.
PREP TIME: 15 minutes
NUTRITIONAL QUOTIENT IN 2 TABLESPOONS FOR A BABY = 1 whole grain, 1 protein, some fruit

Makes about 2 cups

An ideal cereal for the baby who has been exposed to a variety of grains. This recipe makes a storable cereal for you to use at a later time.

1   cup rolled oats
1   cup uncooked brown rice
1/2   cup wheat germ
1   cup banana chips (unsweetened)

Process the oats and rice in a blender until a fine powder results. Add wheat germ and banana chips and process until texture is uniform. To prepare cereal for baby, combine 2 tablespoons granola mixture with 1/3 cup milk in a small saucepan. Simmer for 10 minutes. Put in a bowl and add 1/2 cup milk (or to taste). When used as a topping, this granola adds interest, flavor, and nutrition to yogurt and fruit purees.

EASY FRENCH TOAST

TODDLER RATING: 10 out of 10
PREP TIME: 8 minutes
NUTRITIONAL QUOTIENT IN 1 SLICE = 1 whole grain, 1 protein

Makes 1 slice

This French toast has added toddler appeal because of the surprise taste treat of cinnamon and vanilla. Great for finicky eaters at any meal!

1   slice thin whole grain bread
1   egg, lightly beaten
A pinch of cinnamon
2   drops of vanilla extract

Coat a small frying pan with vegetable spray, then begin heating it over medium heat. In a small bowl, combine the ingredients, except the bread. Dip the bread in this mixture until as much of the egg as possible is absorbed. Move the bread immediately to the frying pan, and heat until the underside is golden brown. Flip and brown on the remaining side. Top with unsweetened applesauce or any of the sauces or syrups in chapter 7.

APPLE OATS

Toddler rating: 9 out of 10
Prep time: 12 minutes
Nutritional quotient in ½ cup =
2 whole grain, 1 calcium, ½ fruit,
¾ protein

Makes 2 cups

Here's a wonderful cereal that makes a great lunch when topped with a swirl of yogurt and some raisins.

$1^3/_4$ cups water
$^1/_3$ cup apple juice concentrate, thawed
$^2/_3$ cup rolled oats
$^1/_2$ cup diced fruit of choice
$^2/_3$ cup nonfat dry milk powder
$^1/_4$ cup wheat germ
A pinch of nutmeg or cinnamon

In a saucepan, boil together the water and juice concentrate. Stir in the oats and cook over low heat for 5 minutes. Add the fruit and cook for 5 more minutes. Add the milk powder, wheat germ, and spice, stirring until the milk powder is dissolved. Serve hot with cold milk. Save leftovers to serve cold topped with yogurt or unsweetened applesauce.

MAKE-YOUR-OWN PUFFED RICE CEREAL

Toddler rating: 10 out of 10

This cereal is made over a period of a few days, and yields about two quarts of homemade puffed rice cereal for snacks and breakfasts. It is a whole grain cereal with no additives.

1 cup raw brown rice
2 cups water
1 quart soy or sesame oil

Simmer 1 cup raw brown rice with 2 cups water for about 45 minutes over low heat. Do not stir. Spread the rice out in a single layer and let it dry for 3 days at room temperature, turning occasionally. Once it dries and hardens, heat the oil to 350° in a deep fat fryer. Lower the rice $^1/_4$ cup at a time into the oil, using a bin or sieve. Fry about 20 seconds, until golden brown. Drain on paper towels. Store in an airtight container.

PILGRIM PANCAKES

TODDLER RATING: 9 out of 10
PREP TIME: 10–12 minutes
NUTRITIONAL QUOTIENT IN TWO 4-
INCH PANCAKES = 1 whole grain,
some calcium, some protein, some
yellow vegetable

Makes about eight 4-inch pancakes

These are quite filling and packed with vitamins A and B. They have a delicious blend of textures and flavors that young children in particular enjoy. Toddlers love to eat these with their hands!

$^1/_2$ cup whole wheat flour
$^3/_4$ cup cornmeal
3   teaspoons low-sodium baking powder
$^1/_2$ teaspoon baking soda
$^1/_4$ cup wheat germ
$1^1/_2$ cups whole milk
$^1/_2$ cup cooked, unsweetened pumpkin
1   egg, lightly beaten
1   tablespoon vegetable oil

Combine the flour, cornmeal, baking powder, baking soda, and wheat germ in a mixing bowl. In a separate bowl, combine the remaining ingredients and mix until smooth. Add the liquid to the dry ingredients and mix thoroughly. Coat a griddle with vegetable spray and heat to medium high. Drop batter by the spoonful to make 4-inch pancakes. Heat until the surface bubbles and the bottoms are golden brown. Turn and brown the remaining side. Top with any of the sauces or syrups in chapter 7 or with apple butter.

BROWN RICE SPOON BREAD

TODDLER RATING: 8 out of 10
PREP TIME: 10 minutes, plus 1 hour 20 minutes to bake
NUTRITIONAL QUOTIENT IN 1 SERVING = some whole grain, some protein, some calcium

Makes about 8 toddler servings

A tasty whole grain addition to your family's menu, this spoon bread has a full-bodied flavor that makes it delicious on a cold winter Saturday morning.

$1/4$ cup cornmeal
$1^1/2$ tablespoons wheat germ
1 tablespoon whole wheat flour
$1/2$ cup cold water
$1/2$ cup boiling water
1 cup cooked brown rice (about $1/3$ cup before cooking)
1 tablespoon vegetable oil
2 eggs, separated
1 cup milk

Preheat the oven to 350°. In a saucepan, bring $1/2$ cup water to a boil. Mix the cornmeal, wheat germ, and flour with the cold water in a separate bowl. Add it to the boiling water and cook for 3 minutes, stirring constantly. Add the rice and the oil. Mix well. Beat the egg yolks with the milk. Beat the egg whites until stiff. Stir the yolk-milk mixture into the hot mixture, then fold in the egg whites. Spray a 2-quart baking dish with vegetable cooking spray. Turn the mixture into it. Set the dish in a shallow pan of hot water and bake for about 1 hour and 20 minutes, until set. Cool slightly. Serve topped with margarine in a small dish.

NOODLE APPLE KUGEL

TODDLER RATING: 10 out of 10
PREP TIME: 30 minutes plus 1 hour
to bake
NUTRITIONAL QUOTIENT IN 1
SQUARE = 1 calcium, $^1/_2$ protein

Makes about 36 squares

This wonderful dish has an appealing, traditional flavor that makes it a great meal for the entire family!

6   ounces egg noodles, medium width
3   eggs, beaten
2   medium apples, peeled, cored, and chopped
$^1/_4$ cup apple juice concentrate, thawed
1   cup plain yogurt
1   cup milk
1   teaspoon vanilla extract
1   tablespoon margarine, melted
1   cup low-fat ricotta cheese (or cottage cheese)
$^1/_4$ teaspoon cinnamon

Preheat oven to 350°. Cook noodles according to package directions. Spray an 8 x 8 baking pan with vegetable cooking spray. In a mixing bowl, combine the eggs, apples, juice concentrate, yogurt, cinnamon, milk, vanilla, and margarine. Add the cheese and mix thoroughly. Fold in the cooked noodles, being careful not to break them up too much. Cover with foil and bake 50–60 minutes. Cool slightly and cut into squares. Serve warm.

BROILED BANANA-CHEESE SPREAD

TODDLER RATING: 9 out of 10
PREP TIME: 5 minutes
NUTRITIONAL QUOTIENT IN 2 TABLESPOONS = $1/2$ calcium, some fruit, some protein

Makes 1 toddler sandwich

An unusual but tasty medley of flavors combines with whole grain goodness in this easy-to-make meal.

1   **medium banana**
$1/2$ **cup grated mild cheese (mozzarella, muenster, mild cheddar)**
$1/4$ **cup wheat germ**
$1/4$ **teaspoon lemon juice**
1   **slice whole grain bread**

Mash the banana with a fork in a small bowl. Add the remaining ingredients and mix thoroughly. Spread 2 tablespoons of the mixture on a slice of whole grain bread or toast. Broil until the cheese begins to melt. Cool slightly. Cut into bite-sized pieces.

SUPER SPREADWICHES

Here are some simple ways to use what you already have on hand to add variety and interesting textures to toddler lunches!

Add any of the following spreads to whole grain bread or toast, whole grain bagels, pita bread, or English muffins for delicious and nutritional results:

Take 2 tablespoons of: peanut butter, cream cheese, yogurt, apple butter, ricotta cheese, mashed hard boiled egg, or cottage cheese.

Add 1 tablespoon (or however much you prefer) of any of the following: wheat germ, raisins, crushed pineapple, unsweetened fruit jam, nonfat dry milk powder, banana slices, rolled oats, chopped dates, grated carrots, or diced apple pieces.

Mix to a spreadable consistency and you have a *Super Spreadwich.*

FESTIVE VEGGIE CRUNCH

TODDLER RATING: Varies greatly, but those who have been introduced to vegetables give it a 9.
PREP TIME: 10 minutes

Makes 3 cups

Best served very cold, with nice crisp vegetables that teethers in particular like to gnaw on. A refreshing and nutritious summer lunch!

1	cup grated carrots
1/2	cup finely chopped raw broccoli
1/3	cup ground sesame seed
1	diced tomato
1/2	cup diced cucumber
1/4	cup diced green pepper
1/4	cup diced celery
1/2	cup of a light Italian salad dressing (optional)

Combine vegetables in a large bowl. When ready to serve, portion into a small bowl or container. Dressing should be added just prior to eating. An easy addition to lunch boxes if you buy individual servings of dressing at grocery stores, or use small airtight containers for lunch box storage.

COTTAGE CHEESE CUPS

TODDLER RATING: 8 out of 10
PREP TIME: 10 minutes
NUTRITIONAL QUOTIENT IN 1
SERVING = $1^1/_2$ protein, 1 whole
grain, 1 fruit, vitamin C (depending on fruit selected)

Makes 1 serving

The perfect, lightly sweet mini-meal for toddlers who have started eating finger foods. Be forewarned: They make quite a mess gobbling it up!

$^1/_4$ cup sliced fruit
$^1/_4$ cup low-salt cottage cheese
1 tablespoon sour cream (optional)
2 tablespoons fruit jam (unsweetened)
1 tablespoon wheat germ

On a small plate, place a scoop of cottage cheese. Surround with fruit, top with jam and wheat germ (and sour cream if under two, for a healthy bit of fat to fulfill nutritional requirements).

MIXED UP LUNCH

TODDLER RATING: 9 out of 10
PREP TIME: 5 minutes
NUTRITIONAL QUOTIENT IN 1 CUP =
1+ fruit, $^1/_2$ iron, some calcium

Makes about $1^1/_2$ cups

An easy blender lunch that many parents can't resist!

1 banana
1 apple, peeled, cored, and sliced
1 pear, peeled, cored, and sliced
$^3/_4$ cup orange juice
$^1/_4$ cup nonfat dry milk powder
2 tablespoons raisins
1 small orange, sliced into wedges

Blend all ingredients except orange wedges in a blender until smooth. Pour into a small bowl or kid-sized cup. Garnish the edge of the bowl or cup with several orange wedges to add appeal.

CRISPY BAKED CARROT STIX

TODDLER RATING: varies greatly
PREP TIME: 25 minutes plus 15 minutes to bake
NUTRITIONAL QUOTIENT IN 1 CARROT STICK = 1 yellow vegetable, some protein

Makes 8 carrot sticks

These easy-to-hold toasted carrot sticks are a welcome side dish on most toddlers' dinner plates. They make a nice lunch dish, too.

2   carrots, scrubbed and cut into quarters
2   tablespoons apple juice concentrate, thawed
1   tablespoon margarine, melted
1   cup wheat germ
1   cup water

Preheat oven to 350°. In a small saucepan, heat water to boiling. Reduce heat and add carrot pieces. Simmer carrots over low heat for about 15 minutes. Drain carrots. Coat carrots with juice concentrate and roll in wheat germ. Coat baking pan with melted margarine and place carrots on pan. Bake for 15 minutes to toast. Cool to safe temperature before serving.

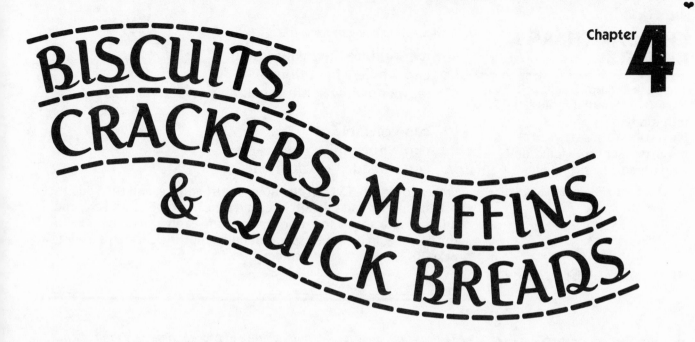

Chapter 4

BISCUITS, CRACKERS, MUFFINS & QUICK BREADS

If your children are like most, biscuits, crackers, and muffins are a wonderful treat. Parents of finicky eaters in particular often search for alternatives to store-bought muffins and crackers that are lacking in nutrition and are filled with preservatives, sugars, and salt.

Here are nutritious alternatives! For quick meals, there are *Cheddar Charms Drop Biscuits* spread with *Ambrosia Apricot Filling* and *Positively Peanut Butter Muffins*. When you have more time, there are *Pumpkin Bread* and *Golden Orange Biscuits*.

Crackers are another ideal lunch box companion and making them yourself allows you to control the ingredients. Toddlers love *Dinosaur Sesame Thins* or *Wheat Germ Crisps* spread with *Homemade Peanut Butter*! Look over chapter 7

for the spreads that will add variety, flavor, and nutrition to these homemade goodies.

Naturally sweetened muffins and quick breads are the ideal snacks. Busy parents can make up a batch on the weekend, then freeze them individually to use for the next month in packed lunches. From *Whole Grain Banana Mini-Muffins* to *Zappers Zucchini Bread*, these treats add nutrition to your toddler's meals without adding refined sugar. And they taste so good that kids look forward to seeing them in their lunches!

Note that it is critical not to overmix muffin batters to prevent them from becoming very tough. Mix the batter just enough to combine the ingredients. The results will be tender and delicious.

CHEDDAR CHARMS BISCUITS

TODDLER RATING: 10 out of 10
PREP TIME: 8 minutes plus 10–12
minutes to bake
NUTRITIONAL QUOTIENT IN 2
BISCUITS = some calcium, some
whole grain, some protein

Makes about 12 large biscuits

A cheese lover's dream come true!

1½ cups unbleached white flour
½ cup whole wheat flour
4 teaspoons low-sodium baking powder
A pinch of salt
⅓ cup vegetable oil
⅔ cup whole milk
½ cup shredded cheddar cheese

Preheat oven to 475°. Sift the flours together once, and then add the baking powder and salt. Sift a second time. Add the oil, cheese, and milk, and stir with a fork until the mixture easily leaves the sides of the bowl. Drop by the teaspoonful onto a nonstick baking sheet. Bake 10–13 minutes until golden brown.

OATS & BUTTERMILK DROP BISCUITS

TODDLER RATING: 10 out of 10
PREP TIME: 8 minutes plus 12–15
minutes to bake
NUTRITIONAL QUOTIENT IN 2
BISCUITS = ½ whole grain, some
calcium

Makes about 10 small biscuits

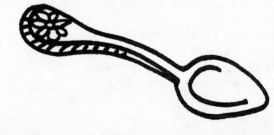

The oat flour adds a nice, nutty change of pace to these easy drop biscuits.

1 cup oat flour (whole grain)
A pinch of salt
3 teaspoons low-sodium baking powder
2 tablespoons margarine
½ cup buttermilk
1 egg

Preheat oven to 425°. Sift together the oat flour, salt, and baking powder into a mixing bowl. With two knives or a pastry cutter, cut the margarine into the dry ingredients until a mealy texture results. In a small bowl, use a fork to beat together the buttermilk and egg. Stir milk mixture into the flour mixture just enough to moisten it. If needed, add more milk by the teaspoonful until the dough is soft but firm. Drop by the teaspoonful onto a nonstick baking sheet. Bake 12–15 minutes until golden brown.

GOLDEN ORANGE BISCUITS

Toddler rating: 10 out of 10
Prep time: 25 minutes plus 10–15 minutes to bake
Nutritional quotient in 1 biscuit = $2/3$ whole grain, some protein

Makes 12 biscuits

The light citrus flavor of these whole grain biscuits will win over the whole family (and friends, too!).

$2/3$ cup whole wheat flour
$2/3$ cup unbleached white flour
3 teaspoons low-sodium baking powder
A pinch of salt
$1/2$ cup wheat germ
1 teaspoon grated orange peel
5 tablespoons cold margarine
$2/3$ cup orange juice concentrate
1 tablespoon apple juice concentrate

Preheat oven to 425°. Sift together the flours, baking powder, and salt into a mixing bowl. Add the wheat germ, orange peel, and margarine; cut these ingredients into the dry ingredients until the texture resembles meal. Stir in the juice concentrates, making the dough smooth and soft. Add water by the teaspoonful if necessary to smooth out dough. Lightly flour a board or counter. Turn out the dough and knead it for 30 seconds. Roll out to about 3/4-inch thick. Cut 2-inch rounds with a biscuit cutter or glass. Cook on a nonstick baking sheet about 10–15 minutes, until golden brown.

DINOSAUR SESAME THINS

TODDLER RATING: 8 out of 10
PREP TIME: 20–25 minutes plus 15 minutes to bake
NUTRITIONAL QUOTIENT IN 2 CRACKERS = some protein, some fruit

Makes about 30 crackers

Use small, dinosaur-shaped cookie cutters to create fun shapes!

2 cups unbleached white flour
1/3 cup vegetable oil
1/4 cup unsweetened fruit juice
1 cup sesame seeds
1/2 teaspoon salt (optional)

Preheat oven to 325°. Combine flour and oil in a mixing bowl. Gradually add the fruit juice, stopping when the dough is soft and easy to work with. Add sesame seeds (and salt, if desired). Mix thoroughly by hand. Roll on a floured surface to 1/2-inch thickness and cut into 2-inch shapes. Place on nonstick baking sheets and poke twice with a fork. Bake 20 - 25 minutes until edges brown.

WHEAT GERM CRISPS

TODDLER RATING: 9 out of 10
PREP TIME: 15 minutes plus 15 minutes to bake
NUTRITIONAL QUOTIENT IN 2 WAFERS = some protein

Makes about 15 wafers

Crispy, nutty wafers that are especially tasty topped with banana slices.

1/2 cup unbleached white flour
2 1/2 teaspoons low-sodium baking powder
3/4 cup wheat germ
1/2 teaspoon salt (optional)
2 tablespoons cold margarine
1/4 cup cold water

Preheat oven to 350°. Sift together into a bowl the flour, salt (if desired), and baking powder. Add 1/2 cup of the wheat germ. Cut in the margarine with 2 knives or a pastry knife. Stir in the water, mixing gently. Roll the dough into a ball and turn onto a floured surface. Roll to 1/2-inch thickness. Sprinkle with the remaining wheat germ, then continue to roll dough until it is wafer thin. Cut into 2" wafers and put on a nonstick baking sheet. Bake about 15 minutes until golden brown.

CRISPY GRAHAMS

TODDLER RATING: 8 out of 10
PREP TIME: 20 minutes plus time
to bake
NUTRITIONAL QUOTIENT IN 1
CRACKER = $^1/_2$ whole grain

Makes 12 crackers

The graham flour in these crackers adds a distinctive nutty and crunchy appeal.

2	cups whole wheat graham flour
1	cup margarine
1	teaspoon baking soda
1	teaspoon cream of tartar
1	egg, lightly beaten
$^1/_4$	cup apple juice concentrate, thawed
$^1/_4$	cup hot water

Preheat oven to 350°. Place whole wheat flour in a large bowl. Cut in the margarine until the consistency of meal is achieved. Add the baking soda, cream of tartar, juice concentrate, egg, and enough water to make a dough that can be rolled thin. Roll out the dough to $^1/_8$-inch thickness on floured surface. Cut into 4-inch squares. Bake on a nonstick baking sheet for 15 minutes, until beginning to brown at the edges. Cool completely before serving.

SWEET WHOLE WHEAT CRACKERS

TODDLER RATING: 9 out of 10
PREP TIME: 12 minutes plus 10 minutes to bake
NUTRITIONAL QUOTIENT IN 4 CRACKERS = $1/2$ whole grain

Makes about 50 crackers

A good multipurpose cracker that travels and freezes well.

2 cups unbleached white flour
2 cups whole wheat flour
1 cup unsweetened fruit juice
$1/3$ cup vegetable oil
A pinch of salt

Preheat oven to 375°. In a mixing bowl combine 1 cup white flour, 1 cup whole wheat flour, fruit juice, salt, and oil until smooth. Add $1/4$ cup at a time of each remaining flour, using only enough flour to form a soft dough consistency. Roll half at a time on a floured surface to $1/8$-inch thickness. Cut with cookie cutters and place on nonstick baking sheets. Bake 9–11 minutes until the edges begin to brown.

RICH AND THIN OAT CRACKERS

TODDLER RATING: 9 out of 10
PREP TIME: 12 minutes plus 8–10 minutes to bake
NUTRITIONAL QUOTIENT IN 4 CRACKERS = 1 whole grain, $1/2$ protein

Makes about 50 crackers

Full of whole grain goodness, these crackers are great with Yogurt-Dill Spread!

$3/4$ cup whole wheat flour
$2/3$ cup wheat germ
$1/2$ cup rolled oats
$1/3$ cup margarine, melted
About $1/3$ cup water

Preheat oven to 375°. Combine flour, wheat germ, and oats in a mixing bowl. Add melted margarine and water gradually, until the dough forms a ball. Roll dough to an $1/8$-inch thickness on a floured surface, then cut into $1^1/2$-inch pieces. Bake until lightly browned, about 8–10 minutes.

QUICK PEANUT CRACKERS

TODDLER RATING: 8 out of 10
PREP TIME: 12 minutes plus 11–13
minutes to bake.
NUTRITIONAL QUOTIENT IN 4
CRACKERS = $^1/_2$ protein

Makes about 45 crackers

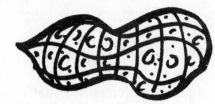

Easy to make and full of protein!

1	cup unbleached white flour
2	tablespoons vegetable oil
2	tablespoons peanut butter
$^1/_4$	cup wheat germ
$^1/_3$	cup milk

Preheat oven to 325°. In a mixing bowl, combine flour, wheat germ, oil, and peanut butter. Gradually add milk until the dough is soft. Knead for about 5 minutes, then roll onto a floured surface to a 1/8-inch thickness. Cut into 2-inch shapes, then place on a nonstick baking sheet. Prick once with a fork, then bake 11 - 13 minutes, until lightly browned.

CRISPY TART CRACKERS

TODDLER RATING: varies greatly.
PREP TIME: 12 minutes plus about
10 minutes to bake
NUTRITIONAL QUOTIENT IN 2
CRACKERS = some calcium, some
protein

Makes about 36 crackers

*These seem to be most enjoyed when spread with **Raisin-Coconut Spread** or **Homemade Peanut Butter**.*

1	cup oat flour
2	tablespoons vegetable oil
1	teaspoon lemon juice

About $^1/_3$ cup yogurt

Preheat oven to 325°. Combine flour, lemon juice, and oil, then gradually add yogurt until a soft dough is formed. Knead for 2 minutes, then roll out on a floured surface to a $^1/_8$-inch thickness. Cut to desired 2-inch shapes; place on nonstick baking pans. Prick once with a fork and bake about 10 minutes, until lightly browned.

PETER'S FAVORITE MINI-MUFFINS

TODDLER RATING: 8 out of 10
PREP TIME: 15 minutes plus 10–13 minutes to bake
NUTRITIONAL QUOTIENT IN 2 MINI-MUFFINS = 1 yellow vegetable, 1 whole grain, 1 fruit, some protein

Makes 4 dozen mini-muffins.
(To make 24 regular-sized muffins, bake 15–20 minutes.)

Younger kids especially love these because they seem perfectly sized for their hands.

1$\frac{1}{2}$ cups apple juice concentrate
$\frac{1}{4}$ cup vegetable oil
2   whole eggs
4   egg whites
1$\frac{1}{2}$ cups canned pumpkin (unsweetened)
1$\frac{1}{2}$ cups raisins
1$\frac{1}{2}$ cups whole wheat flour
$\frac{1}{2}$ cup wheat germ
4$\frac{1}{2}$ teaspoons low-sodium baking powder
2   teaspoons cinnamon

Preheat oven to 375°. In a blender jar, combine juice concentrate, oil, eggs, egg whites, raisins, and pumpkin. Blend on medium until raisins are chopped, 30–45 seconds. In a large mixing bowl, mix flour, baking powder, wheat germ, and cinnamon. Slowly add $\frac{1}{3}$ pumpkin mixture at a time, mixing slowly just until combined. Do not overmix. Either spray muffin tin with vegetable cooking spray or line with muffin cups. Fill each cup $\frac{2}{3}$ full. Bake 10–13 minutes, until tops spring back at your touch. Lightly respray muffin pan for successive batches until batter is finished. Cool on a wire rack.

POSITIVELY PEANUT BUTTER MUFFINS

TODDLER RATING: 9 out of 10
PREP TIME: 15 minutes plus about 15 minutes to bake
NUTRITIONAL QUOTIENT IN 1 MUFFIN = $1/2$ protein, some fruit, some calcium

Makes 12 muffins

Top with a naturally sweet spread like Ambrosia Apricot Filling or Carob Frosting for optimum flavor.

1/4   cup mashed banana
1/4   cup natural peanut butter
2   eggs
1/3   cup vegetable oil
1   cup milk
1/4   cup apple juice concentrate, thawed
1/4   cup wheat germ
1/4   cup nonfat dry milk powder
2   cups unbleached white flour
1 1/2 teaspoons low-sodium baking powder
1   teaspoon baking soda
1   cup chopped peanuts
      (optional, depending on age of child)

Preheat oven to 350°. In a mixing bowl, beat together the banana, peanut butter, eggs, and milk powder until creamy. Add the oil, milk, and juice concentrate and blend well. Stir in flour, wheat germ, baking powder, and baking soda. Add nuts if desired. Either coat muffin pan with vegetable cooking spray or line with muffin cups. Fill each cup 2/3 full. Bake 13–16 minutes, until browned and an inserted toothpick comes out clean. Cool. Add topping or spread before serving.

WHOLE GRAIN BANANA MINI-MUFFINS

TODDLER RATING: 10 out of 10
PREP TIME: 15 minutes plus 10–15 minutes to bake
NUTRITIONAL QUOTIENT IN TWO MINI-MUFFINS = 1 whole grain, some protein, $1/2$ fruit, some iron

Makes about 36 mini-muffins (To make regular-sized muffins, increase baking time to 20–25 minutes.)

An all-natural favorite with nearly every toddler!

1 cup sifted unbleached white flour
1 cup whole wheat flour
$1/3$ cup wheat germ
A pinch of salt
3 teaspoons low-sodium baking powder
1 egg
$1/4$ cup apple juice concentrate, thawed
1 cup milk
3 teaspoons melted margarine
$1/2$ cup mashed ripe bananas
$1/4$ cup raisins

Preheat oven to 400°. In a mixing bowl, combine flours, wheat germ, salt, and baking powder. In a separate bowl, beat together the egg, juice concentrate, milk, margarine, and banana. Add the milk mixture to the dry ingredients and mix until just combined. Fold in the raisins, being careful not to overmix. Either spray muffin pan with vegetable cooking spray or line with muffin cups. Fill each cup $2/3$ full and bake 10–15 minutes, just until done. Great spread with peanut butter!

APPLESAUCE-RAISIN MUFFINS

TODDLER RATING: 10 out of 10
PREP TIME: 15 minutes plus about 12 minutes to bake
NUTRITIONAL QUOTIENT IN 1 MUFFIN = some fruit, some protein, $1/2$ iron

Makes 12 muffins

One of my favorites - light and flavorful.

$1/2$	cup applesauce, unsweetened
$1/2$	cup apple juice, unsweetened
3	eggs
$1/4$	cup margarine, softened
2	cups unbleached white flour
$1/4$	cup wheat germ
1	teaspoon baking soda
3	teaspoons low-sodium baking powder
1	teaspoon nutmeg
$1^1/2$	teaspoons cinnamon
1	cup raisins

Preheat oven to 350°. Combine the apple juice, apple sauce, and raisins in a blender jar. Blend on high until the raisins are completely chopped, about 25 seconds. In a mixing bowl, combine the eggs and margarine, and beat them together on medium. Stir in the raisin mixture. Add the flour, baking soda, baking powder, and spices. Beat just until combined. Either coat the muffin pan lightly with vegetable cooking spray or insert muffin cups. Fill each cup $2/3$ full with batter. Bake 10–12 minutes, just until the tops spring back when lightly touched.

VANILLA CAROB MUFFINS

TODDLER RATING: 8 out of 10
PREP TIME: 12 minutes plus about 15 minutes to bake
NUTRITIONAL QUOTIENT IN 1 MUFFIN = $^1/_3$ fruit, some protein, some whole grain, some iron

Makes 12 muffins

*Especially tasty with a dollop of **Homemade Peanut Butter** and a cold glass of milk.*

$^1/_2$	cup mashed banana
3	tablespoons vegetable oil
1	egg
$^2/_3$	cup milk
$^1/_3$	cup apple juice concentrate, thawed
$^3/_4$	teaspoon vanilla extract
1	cup unbleached white flour
$^1/_2$	cup whole wheat flour
$^1/_4$	cup carob powder
$1^1/_4$	teaspoons baking soda
3	teaspoons low-sodium baking powder
$^1/_2$	cup shredded coconut (optional)

Preheat oven to 350°. Beat together the banana, oil, and egg until creamy. Beat in the milk, apple juice concentrate, and vanilla extract. Stir in remaining ingredients and mix until just combined. Either coat muffin pan with vegetable cooking spray or line with muffin cups. Fill each cup $^2/_3$ full. Bake for 13–15 min, until tops spring back when touched.

MULTIGRAIN CORN MUFFINS

TODDLER RATING: 9 out of 10
PREP TIME: 12 minutes plus 15–20 minutes to bake
NUTRITIONAL QUOTIENT IN ONE MUFFIN = $^1/_2$ whole grain, some protein

Makes 12 muffins

With a hearty buckwheat flavor addition!

$^1/_2$ cup whole grain buckwheat flour
$^1/_2$ cup unbleached white flour
$^1/_2$ cup cornmeal
3 teaspoons low-sodium baking powder
A pinch of salt
2 tablespoons apple juice concentrate, thawed
2 eggs
$1^1/_4$ cups milk
$^1/_4$ cup margarine, melted

Preheat oven to 400°. In a mixing bowl, combine the flours, cornmeal, baking powder, and salt. In a separate bowl, combine the eggs, milk, margarine, and juice concentrate. Add to the dry ingredients and mix just until combined. Either spray the muffin pan with vegetable cooking spray or line with muffin cups. Fill each cup $^2/_3$ full. Bake 15–20 minutes, until an inserted toothpick comes out clean.

BASICALLY BRAN MUFFINS

TODDLER RATING: 8 out of 10
PREP TIME: 12 minutes plus about 12 minutes to bake
NUTRITIONAL QUOTIENT IN 1 MUFFIN = 1 whole grain, $^1/_2$ fruit, some iron

Makes about 18 muffins

*These richly flavored muffins are packed with healthy whole grain and B-vitamins. Spoon on some **Homemade No-Cook Apple Sauce** for a real treat!*

2	cups whole wheat flour
1	cup whole bran cereal (unsweetened) or unprocessed bran
$^1/_4$	cup nonfat dry milk powder
4	tablespoons low sodium baking powder
1	cup milk
$^1/_2$	cup apple juice concentrate, thawed
$^1/_4$	cup vegetable oil
$^2/_3$	cup raisins

Preheat oven to 400°. In a blender jar, combine the milk, juice concentrate, oil, and raisins. Blend on high until the raisins are chopped. In a mixing bowl, combine the flour, bran, milk powder, and baking powder. Slowly add the raisin mixture and stir until just combined. Either coat the muffin pan with vegetable cooking spray or line with muffin cups. Fill each cup $^2/_3$ full and bake 12–14 minutes, until browned and an inserted toothpick comes out clean.

FAVORITE GINGERBREAD

TODDLER RATING: 10 out of 10
PREP TIME: 10 minutes plus 35 minutes to bake
NUTRITIONAL QUOTIENT IN 1 PIECE = $1/2$ whole grain, $1/2$ fruit

Makes an 8 x 8 cake

*This longstanding favorite is even better when topped with **Fruity Whipped Cream** or **Cream Cheese Frosting**!*

$1/2$ cup unbleached white flour
$1/2$ cup whole wheat flour
$1/2$ cup wheat germ
2   teaspoons baking soda
$1^1/2$ teaspoons ground ginger
$1^1/4$ teaspoons ground cinnamon
2   egg whites, lightly beaten
1   cup apple juice concentrate
$1/4$ cup vegetable oil

Preheat oven to 350°. In a large mixing bowl, mix the flours, wheat germ, baking soda, and spices. Stir in the egg whites and $1/2$ cup of juice concentrate. In a small saucepan or the microwave, heat the remaining juice concentrate until hot. Add the hot juice and the oil to the batter, and mix thoroughly. Coat the baking pan with vegetable cooking spray, then pour in the batter. Bake until the top springs back at your touch and the sides begin to pull away from the pan, about 35 minutes. Cool before cutting.

CINNAMON SNACK BREAD

TODDLER RATING: 10 out of 10
PREP TIME: 12 minutes plus about 55 minutes to bake
NUTRITIONAL QUOTIENT IN HALF SLICE = $^1/_2$ protein, some whole grain

Makes one loaf

A nice and easy quick bread that toddlers love to eat plain or lightly spread with soft cream cheese!

3	eggs
$^1/_2$	cup soft margarine
1	cup orange juice
1	cup whole wheat flour
$1^1/_2$	cups unbleached white flour
1	teaspoon baking soda
2	teaspoons low-sodium baking powder
2	teaspoons cinnamon

Preheat oven to 325°. Beat together the eggs, butter, and juice. Add the flours, baking soda, baking powder, and cinnamon. Mix well. Coat a loaf pan thoroughly with vegetable cooking spray. Pour in batter and bake about 55 minutes, until browned, and an inserted toothpick comes out clean.

TODDLER DATE BREAD STIX

TODDLER RATING: 10 out of 10
PREP TIME: 20 minutes plus 45–50 minutes to bake
NUTRITIONAL QUOTIENT IN 1 SERVING = $^1/_2$ whole grain, 1 fruit, $^1/_2$ iron, some protein

Makes 14 date sticks

These deliciously chewy treats keep well for a month in the freezer and for about a week covered, at room temperature.

1$^1/_4$	cups finely chopped dates
1	cup frozen apple juice concentrate, thawed
$^1/_4$	cup vegetable oil
2	egg whites
$^1/_2$	cup whole wheat flour
$^1/_2$	cup unbleached white flour
$^1/_2$	cup wheat germ
1$^1/_4$	tablespoons low-sodium baking powder
1$^1/_4$	teaspoons cinnamon
1	teaspoon vanilla extract

Preheat oven to 350°. In a saucepan, combine dates and juice concentrate, and bring to a boil. Remove from the heat and let cool for 10 minutes. Stir in the oil and allow the mixture to come to room temperature. Thoroughly beat in the egg whites. In a mixing bowl, combine the dry ingredients, and then stir in the date mixture just until combined. Stir in the vanilla. Coat a loaf pan (9 x 5 x 3) with vegetable cooking spray, and then pour in batter. Bake 45–50 minutes, until an inserted toothpick comes out clean. Cool slightly before removing from the loaf pan to a wire rack. When completely cool, slice the loaf into 7 slices, and then halve each slice to yield 14 date bread sticks. Wrap each stick individually and then store in an airtight container.

BUTTERMILK CORNBREAD

TODDLER RATING: 10 out of 10
PREP TIME: 10 minutes plus about 25 minutes to bake
NUTRITIONAL QUOTIENT IN 1 PIECE = 1 whole grain, $^1/_2$ calcium

Makes an 8 x 8 cornbread

A favorite of many families, this easy cornbread is the perfect companion for homemade chili or soup.

1$^3/_4$	cups cornmeal
$^1/_4$	cup whole wheat flour
$^1/_4$	cup nonfat dry milk powder
4	teaspoons low-sodium baking powder
$^1/_4$	teaspoon salt
1	egg, lightly beaten
1	tablespoon apple juice concentrate, thawed
1$^1/_2$	cups buttermilk (If using regular whole milk, add 2 tablespoons vegetable oil to recipe.)

Preheat oven to 425°. In a mixing bowl, combine the cornmeal, flour, milk powder, baking powder, and salt. Add the remaining ingredients and mix just enough to moisten. Coat an 8 x 8 pan with vegetable cooking spray. Turn batter into pan and bake 20–25 minutes, until golden brown on top.

BONGO BONGO BANANA BREAD

TODDLER RATING: 10 out of 10
PREP TIME: 10 minutes plus 45 minutes to bake
NUTRITIONAL QUOTIENT IN 1 SLICE = some fruit, some whole grain, $1/2$ protein

Makes one loaf

Freeze individual slices for easy afternoon or evening snacks.

$3/4$ cup mashed banana
$1/3$ cup vegetable oil
2 eggs
$1/2$ cup apple juice concentrate
1 cup unbleached white flour
1 cup whole wheat flour
$1/3$ cup wheat germ
1 teaspoon baking soda
3 teaspoons low-sodium baking powder
$1/2$ cup raisins
$1/2$ teaspoon cinnamon
$1/2$ teaspoon nutmeg

Preheat oven to 325°. In a blender jar, combine the apple juice concentrate and raisins. Puree until the raisins are completely chopped. Pour this mixture into a large mixing bowl and add the mashed banana, oil, and eggs. Beat thoroughly. Add the flours, wheat germ, baking soda, baking powder, and spices. Mix thoroughly. Coat a loaf pan with vegetable cooking spray and spoon in the batter, spreading it evenly. Bake for about 45 minutes, until an inserted knife comes out clean. Cool completely before slicing.

ORANGE SODA BREAD

TODDLER RATING: 10 out of 10
PREP TIME: 10 minutes plus about 50 minutes to bake
NUTRITIONAL QUOTIENT IN 1 SLICE = some protein, some iron, some fruit

Makes one loaf

A special addition to a St. Paddy's Day dinner or any other special meal!

2   cups unbleached white flour
2   cups wheat germ
4   teaspoons low-sodium baking powder
$1/2$ teaspoon baking soda
$1/2$ teaspoon salt
$1^1/4$ cups raisins
1   tablespoon fresh grated orange rind
$1/4$ cup vegetable oil
1   cup buttermilk
$1/2$ cup orange juice

Preheat the oven to 350°. Oil a $1^1/2$ quart casserole dish thoroughly with vegetable oil. In a large mixing bowl, combine all dry ingredients and mix well. Stir in the remaining ingredients. Turn batter into baking dish and bake 48–52 minutes, until an inserted toothpick comes out clean. Remove from dish to cool on a wire rack.

ZAPPERS ZUCCHINI BREAD

TODDLER RATING: 8 out of 10
PREP TIME: 25 minutes plus about 1 hour to bake
NUTRITIONAL QUOTIENT IN 1 PIECE = $^2/_3$ fruit, $^1/_2$ whole grain, some fat, some iron, some protein

Makes 1 loaf

A lightly flavored loaf that is well worth a little extra time to prepare.

$^1/_2$ cup grated zucchini
1   cup unbleached white flour
$^1/_2$ cup whole wheat flour
$^1/_4$ cup wheat germ
$^1/_4$ cup nonfat dry milk powder
1   teaspoon baking soda
$^1/_3$ cup oil
1   egg
1   can crushed pineapple in juice (8 3/4 ounces)
$^1/_2$ cup raisins

Preheat oven to 350°. Grate zucchini, then dry with paper towels and pack tightly into $^1/_2$ cup. In a mixing bowl, combine the flours, wheat germ, milk powder, and baking soda. In a blender jar, combine the pineapple with juice and the raisins. Blend on high until the raisins are chopped. Add oil and egg to blender and mix on low until combined. Add the pineapple mixture to the dry ingredients in the mixing bowl and mix thoroughly. Stir in grated zucchini. Coat a 9 x 5 x 3 loaf pan with vegetable cooking spray. Pour in batter and bake 60–65 minutes, until an inserted toothpick comes out clean. Cool loaf slightly before removing from pan. Cool completely on a wire rack.

SWEET POTATO OR PUMPKIN BREAD

TODDLER RATING: 9 out of 10
PREP TIME: 20 minutes to make,
75 minutes to let rise, and 35
minutes to bake
NUTRITIONAL QUOTIENT IN 1
SLICE = $^1/_3$ yellow vegetable,
$^1/_2$ whole grain, some protein

Makes 1 loaf

This is worth the extra time it takes. You can tie shoes, put in a load of laundry, or even read a book while the dough is rising.

1   cup unbleached white flour
1   package active dry yeast
A pinch of salt
$^1/_2$ cup milk
$^1/_2$ cup water
$^2/_3$ cup mashed cooked sweet potato or pumpkin
1   tablespoon vegetable oil
$^1/_2$ cup wheat germ
$1^1/_2$ cups whole wheat flour

Mix together the white flour, yeast, and salt. In a small saucepan, heat the milk, water, and sweet potato until very warm. Pour sweet potato mixture into the dry ingredients and mix on medium speed for two minutes. Stir in the oil and wheat germ. Add whole wheat flour by the half-cup until the dough is firm. Knead on a lightly floured surface for 10 minutes until smooth. Oil a large bowl, and turn the dough into it. Flip the dough so that the oil is on both sides. Cover with plastic wrap and allow to rise until doubled, about 45 minutes. Punch the dough down. Oil a loaf pan and turn the dough into it. Allow to rise for 30 minutes. Preheat oven to 375°. Bake for 35 minutes, then turn out and cool on a wire rack.

THIRST QUENCHERS

These easy-to-make beverages are simplicity at its best! From a warm *Touch O' Spice Cider* to an icy cold *Lazy Days Lemonade*, these recipes are a great way to add variety to meals and snacks without sacrificing nutrition. In fact, many of these thirst quenchers are so packed with nutrition that they can easily be an entire snack or small meal unto themselves!

I have found that sometimes the simplest recipe can also be the most successful in terms of taste, nutrition, and convenience. Even a finicky eater will drink an appealingly presented beverage. I know I was delighted when my one-year-old drained a cup of *Fruity Smoothie*. She was getting a serving of calcium plus a serving of fruit, and she loved it!

A wedge of fruit on the side of a cup or a colorful straw makes a big impression on most toddlers, increasing their interest in eating or drinking. You may want to add ice cubes to make some of these beverages extra icy cold, but *only if your toddler is old enough to handle ice cubes without choking*. These thirst quenchers are great, so start experimenting and double the recipes for a treat for yourself, too!

ORANGESICLE SIPPERS

TODDLER RATING: 10 out of 10
PREP TIME: 5 minutes
NUTRITIONAL QUOTIENT IN 1 CUP =
1 vitamin C, $^1/_2$ calcium, some
potassium, 1 fruit

Makes 4 cups

A thirst-quenching, drinkable version of the ice cream confection, without the sugar!

3   cups cold water
$^3/_4$ cup frozen orange juice concentrate, thawed
      (6 ounce can)
$1^1/_4$ cups nonfat dry milk
Medium banana

Blend all ingredients thoroughly in a blender jar. Serve very cold.

TOUCH O' SPICE CIDER

TODDLER RATING: 8 out of 10
PREP TIME: 10 minutes
NUTRITIONAL QUOTIENT IN 1 CUP =
1 fruit

Makes 2 cups

A deliciously warm and mildly spiced addition to a nippy autumn afternoon!

$1^1/_2$ cups apple cider
$^3/_4$ cup water
A pinch of cinnamon
A pinch of allspice
A pinch of nutmeg
Slice of orange for garnish (optional)

In a saucepan, simmer cider, water, and spices together for 10 minutes. Serve warm, garnished with an orange slice to add appeal.

FRUITY SMOOTHIE

TODDLER RATING: 10 out of 10
PREP TIME: 5 minutes
NUTRITIONAL QUOTIENT IN 1 CUP =
1 calcium, 1 protein, 1 fat

Makes 1 cup

Parents rave over this simple way to get their toddlers and older children to drink milk! Even better when served with a wedge of fruit on the edge of the cup.

1   cup milk
$1/4$ to $1^1/3$ cups of a favorite fruit
    (fresh or canned in its own juice)
1   drop vanilla extract
    (optional to add sweetness and flavor,
    usually not needed)

Combine all ingredients in a blender jar and mix on medium until the desired consistency is reached. Often a straw or a wedge of fruit on the edge of a toddler's cup will increase his or her interest.

TODDLER PINA COLADA

TODDLER RATING: 8 out of 10
PREP TIME: 5 minutes
NUTRITIONAL QUOTIENT IN 1 CUP =
some vitamin C, some calcium, 1 fruit, some protein

Makes 1 1/2 cups

Most children find the unusual tropical flavors of this creamy concoction very enticing. A nice and different way to add vitamin C to your child's menu.

$1/2$ cup unsweetened coconut milk
$2/3$ cup unsweetened pineapple juice
1   teaspoon wheat germ
2   tablespoons nonfat dry milk powder

In a blender jar, combine all ingredients and mix until frothy. Best when served very cold.

LAZY DAYS LEMONADE

TODDLER RATING: 8 out of 10
PREP TIME: 5 minutes
NUTRITIONAL QUOTIENT IN
$^1/_2$ CUP = 1 vitamin C, $^1/_2$ fruit

Makes 2 cups

A nice mellow flavor makes this lemonade perfect for young children and parents, too. Because it stores well for up to two weeks, it is convenient to keep on hand for hot summer days.

1   tablespoon lemon juice
2   tablespoons white grape juice
1$^1/_2$ cups cold water

Shake all ingredients together and add ice cubes to chill. Serve cold. (Remove ice cubes if your toddler is not ready for them.)

TWO FRUITY WHIP

TODDLER RATING: 10 out of 10
PREP TIME: 5 minutes
NUTRITIONAL QUOTIENT IN
$^1/_2$ CUP = $^1/_2$ vitamin C, $^1/_2$ fruit, some calcium, some protein

Makes 3+ cups

Toddlers love the flavor combination of orange juice and strawberries! Packed with enough nutrition and taste to make a great lunch for teens and parents, too!

1   cup orange juice
1   cup strawberries (frozen will work if fresh are unavailable)
1   egg
$^2/_3$ cup nonfat dry milk powder
$^1/_4$ cup water

Combine all ingredients in a blender jar and mix until smooth. Serve cold, with a fresh fruit garnish.

TODDLER'S CHOICE THICK FROZEN YOGURT SHAKE

TODDLER RATING: 9 out of 10
PREP TIME: 8 minutes, plus
$1/2$ hour for freezing time
NUTRITIONAL QUOTIENT IN 1 CUP =
1 fruit, 1 calcium, 1 fat

Makes about 2 cups

This shake is so good and so thick that you may decide to serve it for lunch with a few crackers and spread on the side.

1   cup whole milk yogurt
$1/2$ cup each of 3 of your toddler's favorite fruits
     ($1^1/2$ cups fruit total)
2   drops vanilla extract

Combine all ingredients in a blender jar and blend until thoroughly mixed, about 30 seconds depending on the type and consistency of the fruit. Pour into 2 freezer-safe cups. Cover and freeze for 30 minutes. Serve with a spoon. Can be held in the freezer, covered, for up to 2 weeks, then thawed slightly before serving.

TODDLERS' CREAMY EGGNOG

TODDLER RATING: 10 out of 10
PREP TIME: 5 minutes
NUTRITIONAL QUOTIENT IN 1 CUP =
1 calcium, 1+ protein, 1 fat

Toddlers love to join in the festivities with their own version of this traditional holiday favorite. Packed with calcium and lower in fat than the real cream versions, the whole family will enjoy this treat.

2	cups whole milk
1	whole egg
1	egg white
2	tablespoons apple juice concentrate
2	tablespoons nonfat dry milk powder

A pinch of cinnamon
A pinch of nutmeg
1/2 teaspoon vanilla extract

Blend all ingredients except nutmeg in a blender jar until creamy and frothy. Serve cold with a sprinkle of nutmeg on top.

Chapter 6

SNACK TIME

From the simplest *Banana Freezees* to the more complex *Baked Raisin Custard*, here are a multitude of delicious and nutritious sugar-free snacks. *Healthful snacks are more important to toddlers.than to any other age group*, because they eat such a small amount of food that every calorie should be nutritive. Sugary snacks full of empty calories replace nutritious foods for toddlers who do not compensate for junk food by eating more healthy food later. The result is a toddler who has not gotten his or her nutritional requirements.

These healthful snacks allow your toddler to enjoy snacking, which is really just eating a minimeal for a toddler, while getting the nutrition he or she needs.

Children of all ages love to help prepare recipes, and many of these snacks provide the perfect opportunity to involve both younger and older children in cooking, so have fun!

TEETHER BREAD STIX

TODDLER RATING: 9 out of 10
PREP TIME: 15 minutes plus time
to bake
NUTRITIONAL QUOTIENT IN 1
STICK = some yellow vegetable,
some fruit, some protein, $^1/_3$
whole grain

Makes about 32 sticks

You decide how crunchy or soft you want these lightly flavored teething sticks to be!

2   eggs
$^1/_2$ cup apple juice concentrate, thawed
$^1/_2$ cup vegetable oil
$^1/_2$ cup applesauce
$^1/_2$ cup mashed bananas
$^1/_2$ cup grated carrots
$^1/_2$ cup whole wheat flour
$^1/_2$ cup unbleached white flour
3   teaspoons low-sodium baking powder
$^1/_2$ teaspoon baking soda

Preheat oven to 350°. Coat a loaf pan with vegetable cooking spray. In blender jar, combine eggs, apple juice concentrate, and oil. Mix on medium just to blend. Add applesauce, bananas, and carrots; blend well. In a separate bowl, combine the flours, baking powder, and baking soda. Pour in the wet mixture and mix until smooth. Pour into pan and bake about 1 hour, until firm to the touch. Cool completely. Remove from pan. Cut into 8 slices, and then cut each slice into four 1-inch sticks. Lay the sticks on a baking sheet and bake at 150° for 30 minutes (for soft bread-like sticks) or 1 hour (for hard teething biscuits). Store in an airtight container.

WHOLE WHEAT SOFT PRETZELS

TODDLER RATING: 10 out of 10
PREP TIME: 12 minutes, plus 30 minutes to rise, then 15 minutes to bake
NUTRITIONAL QUOTIENT IN 1 PRETZEL = $1/2$ whole grain

Makes about 15 pretzels

A great weekend project which the kids can help with and then eat!

1	cup unbleached white flour
1	cup whole wheat flour
1	tablespoon vegetable oil
1	tablespoon active dry yeast
$3/4$	cup lukewarm apple juice
1	egg

Coarse salt (optional)

Combine $1/2$ cup of each flour with the oil, yeast, and apple juice in a large mixing bowl. Beat with an electric mixer for 3 minutes. Add the remaining flour and knead for 10 minutes, until smooth and elastic. Add more flour if too sticky. Tear off pieces of dough, roll into long snakes and form into desired shapes. Lightly oil baking sheets and place the pretzels on them. Allow to rise in a warm place for 30 minutes. Preheat oven to 450°. Lightly beat the egg and brush onto pretzels. Sprinkle with salt if desired. Bake for 15 minutes until golden brown. Cool to safe temperature before serving.

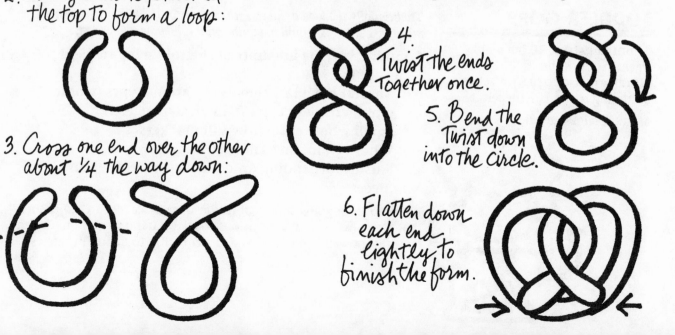

1. form a long snake:

2. Bring ends Together at the top To form a loop:

3. Cross one end over the other about ¼ the way down:

4. Twist the ends Together once.

5. Bend the Twist down into the circle.

6. Flatten down each end lightly to finish the form.

MOM'S FRUITY ICE CUPS

TODDLER RATING: 9 out of 10
PREP TIME: 10 minutes, plus time
to freeze
NUTRITIONAL QUOTIENT IN 1 CUP =
1 fruit, 1 vitamin C (depending on
type of fruit)

An inexpensive and sugar-free alternative to Italian ices.

$^1/_2$ packet unflavored gelatin powder
1 cup fruit juice (except fresh pineapple,
   which will not set up)
1 tablespoon lemon juice
1 cup canned fruit in juice (do not drain)
1 egg white

In a saucepan, combine all ingredients except egg white and bring
to a boil. Remove from heat and allow to cool. Pour into an empty
ice cube tray and freeze until mushy (about 45 minutes). Remove
from freezer. Pour into a bowl and beat until fluffy. Beat egg white
in a separate bowl until stiff; then fold into the icy mixture. Freeze
in ice cube tray until firm. Serve in individual paper cups or small
mugs with spoons.

TODDLER GORP

TODDLER RATING: 10 out of 10
PREP TIME: 5 minutes
NUTRITIONAL QUOTIENT = varies
according to ingredients selected

Makes about 24 servings

*Traditionally the food of hikers, gorp mixes for toddlers are convenient,
nutritious, and tasty (and not quite what a hiker would expect).*

**Combine varying amounts of the following to yield
5 cups of mix:**

> **Natural breakfast cereals of various types (whole
> grain, crispy rice, puffed wheat/rice, etc.)
> Small whole grain, low-salt crackers
> Whole grain, low-salt pretzel pieces
> Raisins (depending on child's age) or other dried fruit
> pieces**

We keep an ongoing supply of this at our day-care center to ensure
that they always have a nutritious snack on hand to give our daughter. It keeps well and can be varied frequently to maintain interest.

JUICE ROCKETS

TODDLER RATING: 10 out of 10
PREP TIME: 10 minutes plus time
to freeze
NUTRITIONAL QUOTIENT IN 1 POP =
1 fruit, 1 vitamin C (depending
on fruit selected)

Makes 6 small pops

Fruit pulp adds fiber to these favorite toddler treats.

1   **cup seedless diced fruit**
1   **cup fruit juice**
1   **cup water**
Small paper cups or Popsicle-style molds
Popsicle-style sticks

Blend fruit, juice, and water in a blender for 20 seconds on high.
Pour into molds, insert sticks, and freeze.

FRUIT LEATHER ROLLS

TODDLER RATING: 8 out of 10
PREP TIME: 15 minutes plus time
to dry
NUTRITIONAL QUOTIENT IN 1
PIECE = some fruit

Makes about 20 pieces

*An inexpensive and healthy alternative to most store-bought, highly
sugared fruit roll-ups. These are easy and fun for the family to prepare.*

Sliced fruit of your choice to make 2 cups of puree
1   **tablespoon lemon juice**
$^1/_4$ **teaspoon ground cinnamon**

Puree sliced fruit. Then, add lemon juice and cinnamon to blender
jar. Blend again. Spread mixture evenly over a 10 x 15 pan. Place in
a 175° oven with the door open for about 3 hours. If bottom is still
wet, flip the leather over and continue to dry. Cut into 20 strips,
and cover each with plastic wrap. Roll up each strip. Store in an
airtight container.

BAKED RAISIN CUSTARD

Toddler rating: 9 out of 10
Prep time: 20 minutes plus 1 hour to bake
Nutritional quotient in 1 serving = $1/2$ calcium, some protein

Makes 6 servings

Preparation must be done one day in advance, but it's well worth the effort. A wonderful treat for special occasions.

2   cups milk
$2/3$ cup raisins
3   eggs, lightly beaten
$1/2$ teaspoon vanilla extract
$1/8$ teaspoon nutmeg plus nutmeg to garnish

The day before you plan to bake the custard, combine the milk and raisins in a container you can cover, and place in the refrigerator. The next day, put the milk-raisin mixture in a blender jar and process until the raisins are finely chopped. Transfer to a large bowl and stir in the eggs, vanilla, and $1/8$ teaspoon nutmeg. Pour into 6 custard cups, stirring frequently to distribute the raisin bits. Sprinkle with additional nutmeg. Preheat oven to 300°. Set the cups in a shallow pan of hot water, so that the water is 1-inch deep around the cups. Bake about 1 hour, until an inserted knife comes out clean. Remove from pan and allow to cool. Chill in refrigerator and serve.

BANANA COCONUT CUSTARD

Toddler rating: 10 out of 10
Prep time: 20 minutes plus 45 minutes to bake
Nutritional quotient in 1 serving = $1/2$ fruit, some calcium

Makes 6 servings

A relatively easy and absolutely delicious treat!

3   eggs
2   bananas, cut in quarters
$1^1/2$ cups milk
1   teaspoon nutmeg
$3/4$ teaspoon low-sodium baking powder
$1/3$ cup unbleached white flour
1   cup flaked coconut (unsweetened)

Preheat oven to 350°. In blender jar, process eggs and bananas on medium until smooth. Blend in remaining ingredients, and then pour into 6 custard cups. Sprinkle tops with nutmeg. Place cups in a shallow pan of hot water to a 1-inch depth. Bake for about 45 minutes, until custard has set in the middle.

REAL GRANOLA BARS

TODDLER RATING: 8 out of 10
PREP TIME: 10 minutes plus time
to set
NUTRITIONAL QUOTIENT IN 1 BAR =
1 whole grain, $1/2$ fruit

Makes 16 bars

Most store-bought granola bars are more akin to candy bars than granola. Here is a healthful and tasty alternative without refined sugar of any type!

3   cups apple juice
$2^1/4$ cups granola (unsweetened)
5   packets unflavored gelatin

In a mixing bowl, combine 1 cup of juice with the gelatin powder. Allow gelatin to soften. Boil 1 cup juice and stir in gelatin liquid until all gelatin is dissolved. Remove from heat. Add the remaining cup of juice and stir in granola. Pour into an 8 x 8 pan and chill until set (2–3 hours). Cut into 16 bars. Wrap individually and store refrigerated. These will hold well in lunch boxes and snack bags.

GRANOLA FOR TOTS

TODDLER RATING: 8 out of 10
PREP TIME: 10 minutes
NUTRITIONAL QUOTIENT IN $1/4$ CUP =
1 whole grain, $1/2$ fruit, 1 iron

Makes 4 cups

Here is a most versatile granola mixture that you can use in muffins, on yogurt, or eat by the toddler fistfuls.

1   cup rolled oats
$1/2$ cup chopped peanuts
1   cup shredded coconut (unsweetened)
1   cup raisins
$1/4$ cup dates
$1/2$ cup sunflower seeds

In a blender jar, process the oats, peanuts, dates, and sunflower seeds until they are chopped to a safe, coarse consistency for toddlers. Add raisins and process briefly (10 seconds). Mix in coconut. Store in an airtight container.

PEANUTTY-BANANA SMOOTHIE

Toddler rating: 10 out of 10
Prep time: 5 minutes
Nutritional quotient in $1/3$ cup =
$1/2$ calcium, 1 fat, $1/2$ fruit, some
potassium, $1/2$ protein

Makes 3+ cups

It seems that anything with peanut butter is a hit with toddlers and this cool smoothie is no exception.

$1/2$ cup natural peanut butter
1   large banana
$1/4$ cup nonfat dry milk powder
$1/2$ cup plain yogurt
$1/4$ teaspoon vanilla extract
4   small kid-sized paper cups

Combine all ingredients in a blender jar and mix on medium for about 20 seconds, until smooth. Pour evenly into paper cups and chill thoroughly. Serve cold.

BAKED APPLE-SPICE HALVES

Toddler rating: 10 out of 10
Prep time: 5 minutes plus 35–40
minutes to bake
Nutritional quotient in 1 half =
1 fruit, some iron

Makes 2 halves

A warm and fruity treat for any cold winter evening. Leftovers are great for breakfast!

1   apple
2   tablespoons apple juice concentrate
$1/4$ teaspoon cinnamon
3   tablespoons boiling water
2   tablespoons raisins (optional)

Preheat oven to 350°. Cut apple in half and remove core. Lay both halves on a baking pan with the skin side down. Spoon 1 tablespoon raisins on the center of each. Combine boiling water, juice concentrate, and cinnamon, then pour this mixture over the apple halves. Bake until tender, 35–40 minutes, basting periodically with its own syrup. Cool to safe temperature and peel off the apple skin before serving.

BANANA FREEZEES

TODDLER RATING: 10 out of 10
PREP TIME: 8 minutes plus time to freeze
NUTRITIONAL QUOTIENT IN 1 STICK = $^1/_2$ fruit, some protein

Makes 4 sticks

Keep a few on hand for those hot summer days when kids don't seem to want to eat "real" food.

2   bananas
4   tablespoons apple juice concentrate, partially thawed
$^1/_4$ cup wheat germ

Peel bananas and cut in half. Insert one Popsicle-style stick into the bottom of each half, so that it stays firmly. Roll in juice concentrate, then coat with wheat germ. Freeze in airtight bags or containers.

FRUIT CREAMSICLES

TODDLER RATING: 9 out of 10
PREP TIME: 8 minutes plus time to freeze
NUTRITIONAL QUOTIENT IN 1 CREAMSICLE = $^1/_2$ calcium, some fruit

Makes 3 pops

Your toddler will be delighted when you join him for a frozen lunch!

1   cup plain yogurt
$^1/_2$ cup chopped fruit

Whip fruit and yogurt in a blender for about 60 seconds. Pour into small paper cups or Popsicle-style molds, insert Popsicle-style sticks, and freeze.

EASY FROZEN YOGURT

TODDLER RATING: 8 out of 10
PREP TIME: 15 minutes plus time to freeze
NUTRITIONAL QUOTIENT IN 1 CUP = $^1/_2$ calcium, some fruit

Makes about 3 cups

A delicious and inexpensive way to help satisfy a toddler's calcium requirement.

1   cup plain yogurt
1   cup fruit slices (bananas, peaches, strawberries, blueberries, and canned pineapple work best)
1   tablespoon white grape juice concentrate

Whip all ingredients together in your blender. Freeze for 30 minutes, then whip again. Repeat 3 more times, and then pour into small paper cups or Popsicle-style molds. Freeze.

HEAVENLY VANILLA ICE CREAM

TODDLER RATING: 10 out of 10
PREP TIME: 10 minutes plus time to freeze
NUTRITIONAL QUOTIENT IN $^1/_2$ CUP = $^1/_2$ fruit, some calcium

Makes 3 cups

What better treat at any time of year than homemade ice cream? And now it can be not only delicious but sugar-free, too.

1   cup milk
2   eggs, lightly beaten
$^1/_2$ cup apple juice concentrate
2   teaspoons vanilla extract
1   cup heavy cream, whipped
$1^1/_2$ cups fruit, peeled, sliced, and frozen

Beat together the milk, eggs, fruit, and juice concentrate. Stir in the vanilla, then fold in the cream. Spoon into an ice cube tray and freeze 45 minutes. Spoon back into mixing bowl and beat until smooth. Return to the ice cube tray and freeze again.

Variations: In place of fruit, add
$^1/_2$ cup carob powder, or
$^2/_3$ cup carob chips, or
$^2/_3$ cup Granola for Tots

FRUIT SHERBET

TODDLER RATING: 10 out of 10
PREP TIME: 10 minutes plus time
to freeze
NUTRITIONAL QUOTIENT IN ½ CUP =
$^1/_2$ fruit

Makes 3 cups

Your toddler can use a spoon to help you chop up the fruit. A great evening or weekend cooking project.

2   cups chopped fruit
14   ice cubes

Puree fruit in a blender. Add ice cubes one at a time and blend until thoroughly crushed. Freeze mixture in an 8 x 8 pan, until sherbet consistency is reached (about 90 minutes). Serve in small cups.

GELLED PICK-ME-UPS

TODDLER RATING: 9 out of 10
PREP TIME: 10 minutes plus time
to set
NUTRITIONAL QUOTIENT IN 1
PIECE $=^1/_3$ fruit

Makes 32 pieces

These juice-based gelatin shapes are stiff enough to be finger food, and will keep for four hours unrefrigerated, making them good lunch box additions.

4   packets unflavored gelatin
1   cup cold fruit juice, unsweetened
3   cups fruit juice heated to boiling, unsweetened

In a bowl, sprinkle the gelatin over the cold juice and allow to stand 1 minute. Add hot juice and stir until gelatin is dissolved. Pour into a 9 x 13 pan and chill until set. Cut into squares, or use cookie cutters to make interesting shapes.

GUMMY CHEWS

TODDLER RATING: 8 out of 10
PREP TIME: 10 minutes plus time
to set
NUTRITIONAL QUOTIENT IN 1
PIECE $=^1/_4$ fruit

Makes an 8 x 8 pan

Inexpensive and healthier than the popular Gummy Bears, which are loaded with sugar, these are chewier than Pick-Me-Ups.

3   cups fruit juice
5   packets unflavored gelatin powder

In a mixing bowl, combine 1 cup juice with the gelatin powder. Bring 1 cup of juice to a boil, then stir in gelatin mix. Add remaining juice and stir until gelatin is dissolved. Pour into an 8 x 8 pan and chill until set. Use cookie cutters or your imagination to cut into dinosaurs, stars, or whatever might strike your toddler's fancy.

HEALTHY GEL

TODDLER RATING: 9 out of 10
PREP TIME: 8 minutes plus time
to set.
NUTRITIONAL QUOTIENT IN $1/8$
PIECE = $1/2$ fruit

Makes 8 x 8 pan

The traditional wiggly dessert favorite, without the added sugar!

2   cups fruit juice (unsweetened)
1   packet unflavored gelatin powder

In a small saucepan, heat one cup juice, then add gelatin powder. Boil, then add remaining juice and stir until gelatin has dissolved. Pour into an 8 x 8 pan and chill to set. Top with *Fruity Whipped Cream* before serving.

MAKE-YOUR-OWN FRUITED YOGURT

TODDLER RATING: 8 out of 10
PREP TIME: 8 minutes
NUTRITIONAL QUOTIENT IN $3/4$ CUP =
1 fruit, 1 calcium

Makes $1 1/2$ cups

An easy and less expensive way to serve your tyke yogurt with fruit. And you control the ingredients!

8   ounces plain whole milk yogurt
$1/2$ cup sliced fruit, drained if canned
2   tablespoons apple juice concentrate
1   tablespoon orange juice concentrate
Dash of cinnamon (optional)

Blend all ingredients together on medium until well mixed and fruit is pureed. Keeps well for two weeks in the refrigerator. Store in individual 4- or 6-ounce containers for sending in lunches.

Chapter 7

SAUCES, SYRUPS & SPREADS

Finally! A wide variety of toppings that add good nutrition as well as that extra flavor or sweetness you sometimes need— without the refined sugar. These sauces and syrups allow you to wean your family from sugar-laden empty calories while adding variety to their meals. The toppings are great on pancakes, waffles, cereals, and fruit. They keep well for up to ten days when refrigerated in an airtight container. Reheat before serving to regain a pourable consistency.

The spreads add versatility and nutrition to breads, biscuits, and crackers. They can turn a ho-hum snack or lunch into something very special. The glazes and frostings allow you to turn muffins, cakes, and quick breads into a cause for celebration, without the refined sugar! You'll be amazed at how many uses you will find for these flavor-packed sugar-free recipes!

CINNAMON CIDER SAUCE

TODDLER RATING: 9 out of 10
PREP TIME: 10 minutes
NUTRITIONAL QUOTIENT IN 2 TABLE-SPOONS = 1 fruit

Makes about 2 cups

This highly flavorful topping can bring the scent of autumn to any season of the year.

1   tablespoon margarine
³/₄ tablespoon unbleached white flour
1¹/₂ cups cider
A pinch of ground clove, cinnamon, or nutmeg (optional)

Melt margarine over low heat. Stir in the flour and simmer for 3 minutes. Add the cider and spices, if desired, and boil together for 2 minutes, stirring constantly.

SWEET RAISIN SAUCE

TODDLER RATING: 8 out of 10
PREP TIME: 20 minutes
NUTRITIONAL QUOTIENT IN 2 TABLE-SPOONS = 1 fruit, 1 iron

Makes almost 2 cups

This topping is a natural with toddlers, who nearly always love the flavor of raisins.

1¹/₂ cups water
¹/₂ cup raisins
¹/₃ cup white grape juice concentrate, thawed
2   tablespoons margarine, melted
³/₄ teaspoon cornstarch

In a blender jar, combine the water and raisins. Blend on high until the raisins are pureed. Transfer to a saucepan and add the juice concentrate. Simmer together for 15 minutes. Add the margarine and cornstarch to the raisin mixture, and bring to a boil, stirring constantly. When the desired consistency is reached, cool slightly and serve over bagels, pancakes, or toast.

PICK-YOUR-FLAVOR JAM SAUCE

TODDLER RATING: 10 out of 10
PREP TIME: 5 minutes
NUTRITIONAL QUOTIENT IN 2 TABLE-SPOONS = $^1/_2$ fruit

Makes almost 1 cup

The speed and ease of this recipe make it a favorite with parents. And children love the variety that you can create with the numerous flavors of sugar-free jams on the market.

$^1/_4$ cup unsweetened fruit jam
$^1/_2$ cup water
$^1/_4$ teaspoon vanilla extract

In a small saucepan, combine the jam and water. Stir and boil together for 2 minutes. Remove from heat and add vanilla. Serve hot or cold on *Hot and Fruity Oatmeal*, *Easy French Toast*, pancakes, or *Heavenly Vanilla Ice Cream*.

GARDEN OF EDEN SYRUP

TODDLER RATING: 9 out of 10
PREP TIME: 10 minutes
NUTRITIONAL QUOTIENT IN 2 TABLE-SPOONS = 1 fruit, 1 iron

Makes about 1 $^1/_2$ cups

A very sweet syrup that most children of all ages love!

6   ounce can white grape juice concentrate
1   cup figs or dates
$^3/_4$ teaspoon cornstarch
$^1/_4$ teaspoon vanilla extract

In small saucepan, combine the juice concentrate and figs or dates. Heat over low heat for 5 minutes to soften the fruit and then pour the mixture into a blender jar. Mix on high for about 1 minute, until the fruit is pureed. Return the mixture to the saucepan. Add the cornstarch and vanilla, and heat over low heat until thickened, stirring constantly. Serve warm.

A TASTE OF AUTUMN PANCAKE SYRUP

TODDLER RATING: 10 out of 10
PREP TIME: 10 minutes
NUTRITIONAL QUOTIENT IN 2 TABLE-SPOONS = $1/2$ fruit

Makes about 2 cups

Keep a batch of this wonderful, sugar-free alternative to maple syrup ready for those weekend waffles or pancakes!

6   ounce can frozen apple juice concentrate, thawed
1   tablespoon cornstarch
1   cup cold water
3   drops maple extract (or to taste)
A pinch of nutmeg (optional)

Mix cornstarch in $1/2$ cup cold water until smooth. In a saucepan, combine the cornstarch liquid, the remaining water, and juice concentrate. Cook over medium heat until the syrup thickens. Stir constantly. When thickened, add the maple extract and optional spice. Serve warm.

SAUCY PINEAPPLE SYRUP

TODDLER RATING: 9 out of 10
PREP TIME: 10 minutes
NUTRITIONAL QUOTIENT IN 2 TABLE-SPOONS = 1 fruit

Makes about $1 1/2$ cups

This chunky syrup is a bright and tasty addition to a plate of warm waffles.

8   ounce can crushed pineapple
$3/4$ teaspoon cornstarch
$1/4$ cup cold water
A pinch of cinnamon

Combine all ingredients in a blender jar and mix on high until pureed. Transfer to a saucepan and cook over medium heat until thickened, stirring constantly. Serve warm.

SURPRISE PRUNE SPREAD

TODDLER RATING: 8 out of 10
PREP TIME: 5 minutes
NUTRITIONAL QUOTIENT IN 1 TABLE-SPOON = 1 fruit, 1 iron

Makes about 1 cup

You'll be surprised how much your toddler will enjoy this iron-rich spread.

1   cup soft pitted prunes
$^2/_3$ cup apple juice concentrate, thawed
$^1/_2$ teaspoon cinnamon

Combine all ingredients in a blender jar and mix until the prunes are pureed. Refrigerate and serve cold.

PEACH TREE SPREAD

TODDLER RATING: 9 out of 10
PREP TIME: 8 minutes plus time for the gelatin to set
NUTRITIONAL QUOTIENT IN 2 TABLE-SPOONS = $^1/_2$ fruit

One of my favorites, this is great on vanilla frozen yogurt!

16   ounce can sliced peaches, packed in juice
1   packet unflavored gelatin
$^2/_3$ cup apple juice, unsweetened
$^1/_4$ teaspoon cinnamon

Drain the juice from the can of peaches into the blender jar. Add the gelatin powder and allow to soften for 2–3 minutes. In a small saucepan, bring the apple juice to a boil and add to blender jar. Blend on high to dissolve powder. Add peaches and cinnamon and blend until smooth. Transfer to a plastic container and refrigerate until set. Allow to come to room temperature for full flavor before serving. An excellent addition to biscuits and bagels.

YOGURT-DILL SPREAD

TODDLER RATING: 8 out of 10
PREP TIME: 5 minutes
NUTRITIONAL QUOTIENT IN 2 TABLE-SPOONS = 1 calcium

Makes about 2 cups

Great in sandwiches and on crackers.

1 cup plain whole milk yogurt
$1/2$ cup cottage cheese
$1/4$ cup shredded mild cheddar
2 tablespoons lemon juice
1 teaspoon dill
$1/4$ teaspoon salt
$1/8$ teaspoon granulated garlic

Combine all ingredients in a mixing bow thoroughly, being careful to distribute the spices. Spread on crackers or sandwiches for a tasty and nutritious lunch or snack.

TWO CHEESE SANDWICH SPREAD

TODDLER RATING: 9 out of 10
PREP TIME: 10 minutes
NUTRITIONAL QUOTIENT IN 2 TABLE-SPOONS = 1 calcium, $1/2$ yellow fruit, some iron

Makes about $3/4$ cup

A rich flavor and chunky texture make this nutrient-packed spread ideal for finicky eaters.

$1/4$ cup cottage cheese
$1/4$ cup shredded mozzarella
2 tablespoons chopped dates
2 tablespoons chopped apricots
2 teaspoons lemon juice

Combine all ingredients in a bowl and mix thoroughly. Spread on sandwiches or crackers.

RAISIN-COCONUT SPREAD

TODDLER RATING: 9 out of 10
PREP TIME: 5 minutes
NUTRITIONAL QUOTIENT IN 2 TABLE-
SPOONS = $1/2$ calcium, $1/2$ iron,
some protein, some fruit

Spread on sandwiches, graham crackers, fruit chunks, or whatever you like!

$1/2$ cup raisins
$1/2$ cup shredded coconut (unsweetened)
$1/2$ cup plain whole milk yogurt
2   tablespoons wheat germ

In a blender jar, combine the raisins and coconut. Blend until the raisins are chopped. Add the yogurt and wheat germ and process briefly, until just combined (about 5 seconds). Enjoy!

HOMEMADE PEANUT BUTTER

TODDLER RATING: 10 out of 10
PREP TIME: 5 minutes
NUTRITIONAL QUOTIENT IN 2 TABLE-
SPOONS = 1 protein, some fat

Makes about $1/2$ cup

As enjoyable to eat as it is easy to make! Plus, it doesn't contain the added salt and sugar of most store-bought brands.

1   cup raw peanuts (or other favorite nuts)
1   tablespoon vegetable oil

Put nuts in a blender jar and blend until very fine. With the blender running, add the oil, and continue to blend until smooth. Store in an airtight container in the refrigerator.

HOMEMADE NO-COOK APPLESAUCE

TODDLER RATING: 10 out of 10
PREP TIME: 10 minutes
NUTRITIONAL QUOTIENT IN ½ CUP =
1 fruit

Makes about 1 cup

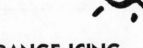

This naturally sweet applesauce keeps well for up to 10 days when stored in an airtight container in the refrigerator. For variety, try different types of apples, or blend to different chunky consistencies.

7   medium sweet apples (Golden Delicious are great)
2   tablespoons apple juice concentrate
Cinnamon to taste (optional)

Wash, peel, and core the apples. Dice into $^1/_8$-inch sized pieces, and put into blender jar. Add the juice concentrate, then blend on high until the desired consistency is reached. Sprinkle each serving with cinnamon, if desired.

ORANGE ICING

TODDLER RATING: 9 out of 10
PREP TIME: 5 minutes
NUTRITIONAL QUOTIENT IN 2 TABLE-SPOONS = some calcium, some fruit, some vitamin C

Makes about 1 cup

Delicious when spread on Peter's Favorite Muffins or Orange-Date Snack Cake!

$^1/_2$ cup nonfat dry milk powder
$^1/_3$ cup orange juice, ice cold

Combine the ingredients in a blender jar and whip on high until stiff. Must be stored refrigerated.

AMBROSIA APRICOT FILLING

TODDLER RATING: 8 out of 10
PREP TIME: 8 minutes
NUTRITIONAL QUOTIENT IN 2 TABLE-SPOONS = 1 yellow fruit, 1 iron

Makes about $^3/_4$ cup

Packed with vitamin A, this is delicious on warm biscuits!

8   whole dried apricots
$^2/_3$ cup raisins
2   apples, peeled and sliced
$^1/_2$ teaspoon cinnamon

In a blender jar, blend the sliced apples about 30 seconds, until liquid begins to form. Add the remaining ingredients and blend until smooth, about $1^1/_2$ minutes. Store refrigerated.

SPICED UP FROSTING

TODDLER RATING: 9 out of 10
PREP TIME: 5 minutes
NUTRITIONAL QUOTIENT IN 2
TABLESPOONS = some calcium,
some fruit

Makes enough to cover 1 bundt-sized cake

A creamy family favorite for birthday cakes in our house.

2	tablespoons soft margarine
2/3	cup nonfat dry milk powder
1/2	teaspoon nutmeg
1	teaspoon cinnamon
1/4	teaspoon allspice
1/4	cup apple juice concentrate
1/4	cup heavy cream
1	teaspoon vanilla extract

Cream together the margarine and the milk powder. Stir in the spices, and then beat in the remaining ingredients until desired consistency is reached. Great on *Carrot Cake!*

CREAM CHEESE FROSTING

TODDLER RATING: 9 out of 10
PREP TIME: 12 minutes, plus 30 minutes for the gelatin to set
NUTRITIONAL QUOTIENT IN 1 TABLESPOON = some calcium, some fruit, some iron

Makes enough to frost two 9-inch layers

A non-traditional version of the carrot cake classic, this frosting will have even diehards thinking it is too delicious to be healthy.

$1/2$ cup apple juice concentrate
16   ounces light cream cheese
2   teaspoons vanilla extract
$2/3$ cup raisins, finely chopped
      (in blender or food processor)
$1^1/2$ teaspoons unflavored gelatin powder

Put 2 tablespoons juice concentrate and the gelatin powder in a small saucepan. Place the remaining juice concentrate, cream cheese, vanilla, and chopped raisins in a blender jar and mix until smooth. Heat gelatin-juice mixture to boiling, stirring to dissolve the gelatin. Transfer the cream cheese mixture to a mixing bowl, and stir in the gelatin mixture, blending well. Refrigerate just until the gelatin starts to set, about 30–45 minutes. Frost the cake.

LIGHT CAROB GLAZE

TODDLER RATING: 8 out of 10
PREP TIME: 5–8 minutes
NUTRITIONAL QUOTIENT =
negligible amounts

Makes about ³/4 cup

For those times when you don't want overpowering flavor, this light glaze is the perfect finish.

1   tablespoon margarine at room temperature
¹/2   cup carob powder
¹/2   cup water
1   teaspoon vanilla extract

Combine all ingredients in a saucepan over medium heat, stirring constantly. When the glaze thickens, drizzle it hot over your cake or pastry. Reheat slightly to use leftover glaze.

CAROB FROSTING

TODDLER RATING: 8 out of 10
PREP TIME: 8 minutes
NUTRITIONAL QUOTIENT IN 1
TABLESPOON= some fruit

Makes about ³/4 cup

Great on Positively Peanut Butter Muffins!

¹/2   cup mashed ripe banana
1   tablespoon margarine
7   tablespoons carob powder
1¹/2 teaspoons vanilla extract
3   tablespoons unbleached white flour

In a large mixing bowl, combine all ingredients and mix on high until smooth.

FRUITY WHIPPED CREAM

TODDLER RATING: 10 out of 10
PREP TIME: 5 minutes
NUTRITIONAL QUOTIENT IN 2 TABLE-
SPOONS = some calcium, some fat,
some fruit

Makes almost 2 cups

*A delicious topping for fruit cups, frozen yogurt, or **Favorite Gingerbread**.*

1/2 cup sliced fruit
1/2 pint heavy cream

In a blender jar, mix the fruit until it has a smooth consistency. Add the cream and whip on high until peaks form. Dollop where you please!

Chapter 8

COOKIES, CAKES & BARS

Every toddler loves a cookie, and now you can have cookies on hand that you actually enjoy seeing your toddler eat! You can choose from the conventional (see *Luscious Lemon Rounds* or *Apple-Raisin Oatmeal Cookies*) or the unconventional-but-still-delicious (see *No-Bake Bumpy Peanut Butter Nuggets* or *Caribbean Refrigerator Cookies*). They all freeze well for up to a month when sealed tightly, and they are all packed with nutrition.

It seems almost too good to be true, but the flavorful cakes and snack bars are indeed free of refined sugar, also. There are any number of treats in store, so take a few moments to bake one of these delights for a family treat.

CARIBBEAN REFRIGERATOR COOKIES

TODDLER RATING: 9 out of 10
PREP TIME: 15 minutes plus 10–12 minutes to bake
NUTRITIONAL QUOTIENT IN 1 COOKIE =1 fruit, some protein, some whole grain

Makes about 5 dozen small cookies

The delicious flavors of pineapple, coconut, and dates combine in these golden brown wonders!

$2/3$ cup margarine
1   egg
2   teaspoons vanilla extract
$1^3/4$ teaspoons low-sodium baking powder
A pinch of salt
$1/2$ cup unbleached white flour
$1/2$ cup whole wheat flour
1   cup chopped dates (unsugared)
1   cup shredded coconut (unsweetened)
$1/2$ cup dried pineapple, chopped (unsugared)
$2/3$ cup wheat germ

In a medium mixing bowl, cream together the margarine, egg, and vanilla. Gradually beat in the baking powder, salt, and flours, mixing thoroughly. Mix in the dates, coconut, and pineapple. Form the dough into 2 logs, about $1^1/2$ inches in diameter. Roll the logs in the wheat germ to coat them. Wrap in waxed paper and chill until firm enough to slice, about 2 hours. Preheat oven to 350°. Slice cookies about $3/8$-inch thick and place on a nonstick cookie sheet. Bake 10–12 minutes until golden brown.

NO-BAKE BUMPY PEANUT BUTTER NUGGETS

Toddler rating: 10 out of 10
Prep time: 10 minutes plus time to chill
Nutritional quotient in 2 balls = $1/3$ whole grain, $1/3$ protein, some fat, some iron, some fruit

Makes 30 small balls

Put these out for birthday party snacking and watch them disappear!

- $1/2$ cup natural peanut butter
- $1/4$ cup nonfat dry milk powder
- $1/4$ cup shredded coconut (unsweetened)
- $1/4$ cup raisins (chopped, if your child is too young to eat whole)
- $1/3$ cup rolled oats
- $1/2$ teaspoon cinnamon
- $1/4$ cup wheat germ
- $1/4$ cup apple juice concentrate, thawed

Combine all ingredients in a large mixing bowl and mix thoroughly. Shape into 1-inch balls. Line up on a cookie sheet or baking pan and chill thoroughly before serving. Store refrigerated.

JESSICA'S SPICE COOKIES

TODDLER RATING: 9 out of 10
PREP TIME: 12 minutes to mix, 2 hours to chill, and 8–10 minutes to bake
NUTRITIONAL QUOTIENT IN 1 COOKIE = 1 whole grain, $^1/_3$ fruit, some iron, some protein

Makes about 24 cookies

My daughter's favorites!

$1^1/_2$	cups whole wheat flour
$^3/_4$	cup wheat germ
$1^1/_2$	teaspoons low-sodium baking powder
1	teaspoon baking soda
$^1/_2$	teaspoon allspice
$1^1/_4$	teaspoons ginger
$1^1/_2$	teaspoons cinnamon
1	cup apple juice concentrate
$^2/_3$	cup raisins
$^1/_4$	cup vegetable oil
2	egg whites

Combine dry ingredients in a mixing bowl. In a blender jar, combine the juice concentrate and the raisins. Mix on high until raisins are chopped. Add the egg whites and beat on slow speed just until combined. Slowly add the juice mixture to the dry ingredients and mix until combined. Wrap the somewhat soft dough in waxed paper and chill for 2 hours. Preheat oven to 375°. Wet your hands and shape the dough into balls which are $1^1/_2$ inches in diameter. Place on a nonstick cookie sheet and flatten with a fork. Bake 8–10 minutes until just done. Don't overbake! Cool on wire rack.

CAROB DROP BROWNIES

TODDLER RATING: 8 out of 10
PREP TIME: 10 minutes plus about 10 minutes to bake
NUTRITIONAL QUOTIENT IN 1 BROWNIE COOKIE = $1/2$ protein, some fruit, $1/2$ whole grain, some iron

Makes about 48 small brownies

Toddlers love to put funny faces on these! As soon as the brownies cool enough to touch after baking, have the children give them eyes, mouths, and noses made with yogurt-covered raisins.

$1/2$	cup mashed banana
$1/3$	cup vegetable oil
$1/4$	teaspoon vanilla extract
2	eggs
$1/4$	cup milk
1	cup unbleached white flour
$1/4$	cup whole wheat flour
$1/4$	cup carob powder
2	tablespoons wheat germ
$1/4$	teaspoon baking soda
$2/3$	cup rolled oats

Preheat oven to 350°. In a mixing bowl, beat together the mashed banana, oil, vanilla extract, eggs, and milk until creamy. Beat in the flours, carob powder, wheat germ, and baking soda. Stir in the oats and mix thoroughly. Coat a cookie sheet with vegetable cooking spray. Drop batter by the teaspoonful onto cookie sheet and bake 8–10 minutes, until just firm to the touch. Don't overbake! Cool before serving for full flavor.

OATMEAL FRUITED COOKIES

TODDLER RATING: 9 out of 10
Prep time: 12 minutes plus 10–12 minutes to bake
NUTRITIONAL QUOTIENT IN 1 COOKIE = some whole grain, $1/2$ iron, $1/2$ fruit

Makes about 24 cookies

Chewy, fruity, richly flavored cookies that are fun to "gum."

10 pitted dates
5 dried figs
$2/3$ cup raisins
$1/3$ cup apple juice concentrate, thawed
$1^1/2$ cups rolled oats
$1/4$ cup wheat germ
1 egg white
$1/4$ cup vegetable oil
A pinch of cinnamon

Preheat oven to 350°. Combine juice concentrate, dates, figs, and raisins in a saucepan and simmer on low for 10 minutes, until fruit softens. Pour this mixture into a blender jar and puree until all the fruit is chopped. Transfer to a mixing bowl. Add the oil, oats, and cinnamon, and mix thoroughly. In a separate bowl, beat the egg white lightly, then fold it gently into the batter. Drop batter by the tablespoonful onto a nonstick cookie sheet. Press flat with a fork. Bake 10–12 minutes until centers are just done. Cool on wire rack.

LUSCIOUS LEMON ROUNDS

TODDLER RATING: 8 out of 10
PREP TIME: 10 minutes plus 7–9 minutes to bake
NUTRITIONAL QUOTIENT IN 1 COOKIE = $1/3$ fruit, some vitamin C, some protein

Makes about 30 large cookies

Big, round cookies with a light lemon flavor.

4	eggs
$1/2$	cup vegetable oil
6	ounces frozen pineapple juice concentrate
$1/3$	cup lemon juice
$1\frac{1}{4}$	cups unbleached white flour
$3/4$	cup whole wheat flour
$1/4$	cup wheat germ
1	teaspoon low-sodium baking powder

Preheat oven to 375°. In a large mixing bowl, beat together the eggs, oil, pineapple concentrate, and lemon juice. Add both flours, wheat germ, baking powder, and beat thoroughly. Drop by the heaping teaspoonful onto nonstick cookie sheets. Bake for 7–9 minutes until tops are firm. Do not brown! Cool slightly and remove from cookie sheets to wire rack.

COCONUT PINEAPPLE COOKIES

TODDLER RATING: 8 out of 10
PREP TIME: 15 minutes plus about 15 minutes to bake
NUTRITIONAL QUOTIENT IN 1 COOKIE = $^3/_4$ fruit, some whole grain, some protein, some fat

Makes about 12 cookies

These naturally sweet and very fruity cookies are moist enough to keep well for two weeks when tightly covered at room temperature.

3   eggs
$^1/_2$ cup margarine, softened
1   can (20 ounces) crushed pineapple in juice
$1^1/_4$ cups water
1   cup whole wheat flour
$1^1/_2$ cups unbleached white flour
$^1/_4$ cup wheat germ
1   teaspoon baking soda
$3^1/_2$ teaspoons low-sodium baking powder
1   teaspoon cinnamon
2   cups flaked coconut

Preheat oven to 375°. Beat together the eggs, margarine, water, and the juice from the can of pineapple (about 1 cup). Beat in the flours, wheat germ, baking soda, baking powder, and cinnamon. Mix thoroughly. Stir in the coconut and the well-drained pineapple. Combine thoroughly. Drop by the tablespoonful onto a nonstick cookie sheet. Bake 12–15 minutes until just browned.

APPLE-RAISIN OATMEAL COOKIES

TODDLER RATING: 10 out of 10
PREP TIME: 20 minutes plus 8–10 minutes to bake
NUTRITIONAL QUOTIENT IN 2 COOKIES = 1+ whole grain, 1 fruit, some iron, $^1/_2$ protein

Makes about 36 cookies

Great nutrient-rich finger foods for those with few teeth. These cookies are also flavorful enough to satisfy older children.

1   cup whole wheat flour
$^3/_4$ cup wheat germ
$^1/_2$ cup rolled oats
1   tablespoon low-sodium baking powder
$1^1/_2$ teaspoons cinnamon
$^1/_2$ teaspoon ginger
1   cup apple juice concentrate, thawed
$^1/_4$ cup vegetable oil
1   egg (or two egg whites for the young child who has not started eating yolks yet)
$^2/_3$ cup raisins
$^1/_4$ cup dried apples

Preheat oven to 375°. In a large mixing bowl, combine the flour, wheat germ, oats, baking powder, cinnamon, and ginger. In a blender jar, combine the juice concentrate, oil, egg, raisins, and dried apples. Blend at medium speed until the raisins and apples are chopped. Stir this juice mixture into the dry ingredients and combine thoroughly. Drop batter by the heaping teaspoonful onto nonstick cookie sheets. Flatten each with a fork, and bake 8–10 minutes until the top springs back at your touch. Do not brown or crisp! Cool slightly before removing from cookie sheets to wire racks.

PEANUT BUTTER FACES

TODDLER RATING: 8 out of 10
PREP TIME: 15 minutes plus 5–8 minutes to bake
NUTRITIONAL QUOTIENT IN 1 COOKIE = $1/3$ protein, $1/3$ fat

Makes about 24 cookies

The flavor of these fun cookies will improve after 24 hours, so they are a good choice to bake ahead of time.

$1^2/3$ cups unbleached white flour
$1/2$ cup natural peanut butter
1 egg, well beaten
$1/4$ cup margarine
$1/2$ cup apple juice concentrate, thawed
2 teaspoons low-sodium baking powder
$1/3$ cup wheat germ
A pinch of salt
$1^1/2$ teaspoons vanilla extract
1 cup raisins

Preheat oven to 400°. Sift together the flour, baking powder, and salt. Cream together the margarine, peanut butter, and vanilla extract. Add the egg and juice concentrate. Blend well. Add the dry ingredients one at a time, mixing well after each addition. Mix in $3/4$ cup of the raisins. Drop by the level tablespoonful onto an ungreased cookie sheet. Flatten each cookie with a fork. Have your toddler help you take the remaining raisins and make funny faces on each cookie. Bake 12–15 minutes until tops just spring back. Cool completely on a wire rack. Store in an airtight container.

NO-BAKE CREAM CHEESE BALLS

TODDLER RATING: 8 out of 10
PREP TIME: 8 minutes plus time to chill
NUTRITIONAL QUOTIENT IN 2 BALLS = 1 calcium, some protein

Makes about fifteen 1-inch balls

A wonderful treat that toddlers seem to really enjoy.

8   ounces cream cheese at room temperature
1   teaspoon vanilla extract
4   teaspoons white grape juice concentrate, thawed
8   teaspoons nonfat dry milk powder
1   cup wheat germ

Mix together thoroughly all ingredients except the wheat germ. Form into 15 balls. Roll each ball in the wheat germ to coat. Chill until firm. Store refrigerated.

CAROB CHIP COOKIES

TODDLER RATING: 8 out of 10
PREP TIME: 12 minutes plus 8–10 minutes to bake
NUTRITIONAL QUOTIENT IN 1 COOKIE = 1/3 whole grain, some protein, some iron

Makes about 24 cookies

A healthy alternative to traditional chip cookies, these carob wonders will become new favorites to many youngsters!

1/4   cup mashed banana
1/4   cup vegetable oil
1/4   cup apple juice concentrate, thawed
1   egg
1   cup unbleached white flour
1/4   cup wheat germ
1   cup rolled oats
3/4   cup carob chips

Preheat oven to 350°. Cream together the mashed banana and oil. Beat in the egg and juice concentrate. Add remaining ingredients and mix well. Drop batter by the heaping teaspoonful onto a nonstick cookie sheet. Bake 8–10 minutes, just until edges start to brown. Cool on wire rack.

APPLECAKE SQUARES

TODDLER RATING: 9 out of 10
PREP TIME: 25 minutes plus about 50 minutes to bake
NUTRITIONAL QUOTIENT IN 1 PIECE = 1 whole grain, $^{1}/_{2}$ fruit, $^{1}/_{2}$ protein

Makes an 8 x 8 cake

These snack squares are so packed with whole grain goodness that you'll be glad to see your toddler ask for one more piece!

$^{3}/_{4}$ cup whole wheat flour
$^{1}/_{2}$ cup wheat germ
$1^{1}/_{2}$ teaspoons baking soda
1   teaspoon cinnamon
$^{1}/_{2}$ teaspoon nutmeg
$1^{3}/_{4}$ cups apple juice concentrate, thawed
$^{2}/_{3}$ cup dried apple pieces, chopped
1   cup rolled oats
$^{1}/_{3}$ cup margarine
1   egg
2   egg whites
1   teaspoon vanilla extract

Preheat the oven to 350°. In a small saucepan, heat the juice concentrate on medium for 5 minutes. In a mixing bowl, combine the flour, wheat germ, baking soda, and spices. In another bowl, cover the rolled oats and apple pieces with the hot juice concentrate. Cover and let stand 20 minutes. Beat the margarine in a bowl at high speed, until it is fluffy. Beat in the egg, egg whites, and vanilla. Add the oat-apple mixture and mix well. Stir in the flour mixture until well combined. Coat an 8 x 8 baking pan with vegetable cooking spray. Pour in the batter and bake until the top springs back at your touch, about 50 minutes. Cool completely before cutting.

CHEESECAKE FOR CHAMPIONS

TODDLER RATING: 9 out of 10
PREP TIME: 15 minutes plus time for the cake to set in the refrigerator
NUTRITIONAL QUOTIENT IN 1 PIECE = $1/2$ protein, $1/2$ fruit, $1/2$ calcium

Makes 1 cheesecake

You will need a 10-inch pie plate for this recipe.

For crust: $1/4$ cup wheat germ
                1 teaspoon ground cinnamon
$2^{1}/2$ tablespoons unflavored gelatin
$1^{1}/4$ cups apple juice concentrate, thawed
1   cup evaporated milk
2   teaspoons vanilla extract
$1^{1}/2$ cups soft cream cheese
$1^{1}/2$ cups pot-style cottage cheese
2   egg whites in 2 tablespoons apple juice concentrate, thawed
$1/4$ teaspoon cream of tartar

Spray a 10-inch pie plate thoroughly with vegetable cooking spray. Mix together the wheat germ and cinnamon for the crust. Sprinkle this mixture over the pie plate, thoroughly coating it, using all of the wheat germ mixture. In a mixing bowl, combine the gelatin powder and $1/2$ cup of the juice concentrate. Set aside and allow the gelatin to soften. In a saucepan, bring the milk to a boil, add the gelatin mixture and stir until the gelatin is dissolved. Add the vanilla extract and $3/4$ cup juice concentrate to the milk mixture. In a blender jar, combine the cheeses and $1/3$ of the milk mixture. Process until smooth. Repeat this process twice more until all of the milk mixture is blended in. Pour into a bowl and chill just until set. Do not allow it to become firm. Add the cream of tartar to the egg whites and juice and beat until stiff. Take the cheese mixture from the refrigerator and quickly fold in the egg white mixture, without deflating the egg whites. Pour into pie plate and chill until firm.

Variations: Add any of the following to the mix when blending in the milk mixture:
$1/2$ cup carob powder
$1/2$ cup well-drained fruit (canned or fresh)
$1/2$ teaspoon almond extract
2   tablespoons fresh grated orange or lemon rind

ORANGE-DATE SNACK CAKE

TODDLER RATING: 8 out of 10
PREP TIME: 15 minutes plus about 35 minutes to bake
NUTRITIONAL QUOTIENT IN 1 PIECE = 1 fruit, 1 fat, $1/2$ whole grain, 1 iron, some calcium

Makes an 8 x 8 cake

The naturally sweet taste of dates combines with a light orange flavor for a real taste treat!

$1/2$ **cup chopped dates (pitted, unsugared)**
$1/2$ **cup nonfat dry milk powder**
$1/4$ **cup softened margarine**
1 **egg**
$3/4$ **cup orange juice**
$1/2$ **cup unbleached white flour**
$1/2$ **cup whole wheat flour**
2 **teaspoons low-sodium baking powder**

Preheat oven to 325°. Cream together the margarine and milk powder. Beat in the egg and orange juice thoroughly, and then stir in the flour and baking powder. Blend well. Add the chopped dates and mix until evenly distributed. Coat an 8 x 8 pan with vegetable cooking spray. Pour in batter and bake until an inserted toothpick comes out clean (30–35 minutes). Cool before slicing.

EGGLESS BABY CAKE

TODDLER RATING: 10 out of 10
PREP TIME: 12–15 minutes
NUTRITIONAL QUOTIENT IN 1
PIECE = 1 fruit, $^{1}/_{2}$ whole grain,
some protein

Makes an 8 x 8 cake

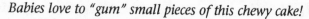

Babies love to "gum" small pieces of this chewy cake!

1 cup apple juice concentrate
$^{2}/_{3}$ cup chopped raisins
$^{1}/_{4}$ cup chopped dried apples
$^{1}/_{4}$ cup margarine
$^{1}/_{2}$ cup whole wheat flour
$^{1}/_{4}$ cup unbleached white flour
$^{1}/_{2}$ cup wheat germ
$4^{1}/_{2}$ teaspoons low-sodium baking powder

Preheat the oven to 325°. In a small saucepan, combine the juice concentrate, dried fruits, margarine, and cinnamon. Simmer over low heat until the margarine melts. Remove from heat and allow to cool. In a mixing bowl, combine the flours, wheat germ, and baking powder. Slowly add the fruit mixture, and stir just until mixed. Coat an 8 x 8 baking pan with vegetable spray and pour in the batter. Bake about 30 minutes, until an inserted toothpick comes out clean. Cool and then cut into 16 squares. For future use, wrap pieces individually and store in the freezer in an airtight container.

PINEAPPLE YELLOW CAKE

TODDLER RATING: 9 out of 10
PREP TIME: 15 minutes plus 35
minutes to bake
NUTRITIONAL QUOTIENT IN 1
PIECE = $^3/_4$ whole grain,
$^1/_2$ protein, $^1/_2$ fruit, 1 iron

Makes an 8 x 8 cake

Babies and toddlers alike enjoy this moist and nutrient-rich cake with its rich, fruity combination of flavors!

$^1/_2$ cup chopped apricots
$^3/_4$ cup crushed pineapple, drained well
2 eggs
$^1/_4$ cup vegetable oil
$1^1/_4$ cups milk
$^1/_4$ teaspoon vanilla extract
$2^1/_3$ cups unbleached white flour
1 teaspoon baking soda
3 teaspoons low-sodium baking powder
$^1/_4$ teaspoon nutmeg
$^1/_4$ teaspoon cinnamon
$^1/_2$ cup flaked coconut (unsweetened)

In a blender jar, combine the pineapple and apricots, and mix on high until smooth. In a large mixing bowl, beat together the eggs, pineapple mixture, oil, milk, and vanilla extract. Add the flour, baking soda, baking powder, and spices, and beat well. Stir in the coconut. Coat an 8 x 8 baking pan with vegetable cooking spray and then pour in the batter. Bake 15–20 minutes, until browned and an inserted toothpick comes out clean. Cool before cutting.

SPECIAL CAROB CAKE

TODDLER RATING: 8 out of 10
PREP TIME: 10 minutes plus about 25 minutes to bake.
NUTRITIONAL QUOTIENT IN 1 PIECE = some fruit, some protein, some iron, some whole grain

Makes a 9 x 13 cake

*Children seem to like diving into this flavorful cake, especially when it is iced with **Carob Frosting**!*

3   eggs
$1/3$ cup mashed banana
$1/2$ cup soft margarine
1   cup milk
$1/4$ cup white grape juice concentrate, thawed
2   teaspoons vanilla extract
$1^1/4$ cups unbleached white flour
1   cup whole wheat flour
$3/4$ cup carob powder
$3^1/2$ teaspoons low-sodium baking powder
1   teaspoon baking soda
1   cup shredded coconut (unsweetened)

Preheat oven to 350°. In a large mixing bowl, beat together the eggs, mashed banana, margarine, milk, and juice concentrate until creamy. Add remaining ingredients except coconut and mix well. Stir in the coconut. Pour batter into baking pan, and bake for 20–25 minutes, until an inserted toothpick comes out clean. Cool before slicing.

PUMPKIN BUNDT CAKE

TODDLER RATING: 9 out of 10
PREP TIME: 12 minutes plus about
1 hour and 20 minutes to bake
NUTRITIONAL QUOTIENT IN 1
PIECE = $3/4$ whole grain,
$1/2$ yellow vegetable, some fruit,
some protein, some iron

Makes one bundt cake or two 9-inch layers

Try spreading slices of this moist, richly spiced cake with an orange marmalade Jam Sauce or Raisin-Coconut Spread.

2   cups apple juice concentrate, thawed
1   cup vegetable oil
2   cups cooked mashed pumpkin (unsweetened)
4   eggs, lightly beaten
3   cups whole wheat flour
1   teaspoon ground cinnamon
$1/2$ teaspoon ground allspice
$1/4$ teaspoon ground ginger
4   teaspoons low-sodium baking powder
2   teaspoons baking soda
2   teaspoons vanilla extract
1   cup raisins

Preheat oven to 350°. In a large mixing bowl, mix all ingredients together thoroughly. Coat bundt pan with vegetable cooking spray and pour in batter. Bake about 1 hour and 20 minutes, until the cake starts to pull away from the sides and the top springs back at your touch. Cool slightly before removing from pan.

SPICED APPLE BARS

TODDLER RATING: 9 out of 10
PREP TIME: 12 minutes, plus about 30 minutes to bake.
NUTRITIONAL QUOTIENT IN 1 PIECE = some fruit, some protein, $^{1}/_{2}$ whole grain

Makes an 8 x 8 cake

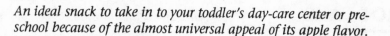

An ideal snack to take in to your toddler's day-care center or pre-school because of the almost universal appeal of its apple flavor.

$^{1}/_{2}$ cup applesauce
$^{1}/_{2}$ cup apple juice
3   eggs
$^{1}/_{4}$ cup margarine
1   cup unbleached white flour
1   cup whole wheat flour
1   teaspoon baking soda
3   teaspoons low-sodium baking powder
$^{1}/_{2}$ teaspoon nutmeg
$1^{1}/_{2}$ teaspoons cinnamon
$^{3}/_{4}$ cup raisins

Preheat oven to 350°. Coat an 8 x 8 pan with vegetable cooking spray. In a mixing bowl, beat together the applesauce, apple juice, eggs, and margarine until well blended. Add the flours, baking soda, baking powder, and spices. Beat for 2 minutes at medium speed. Stir in raisins. Bake 25–30 minutes, until an inserted toothpick comes out clean.

CARROT CAKE

TODDLER RATING: 9 out of 10
PREP TIME: 15 minutes plus about
35 minutes to bake
NUTRITIONAL QUOTIENT IN 1
PIECE = $3/4$ whole grain, 1 yellow
vegetable, 1 fat, 1 fruit, and some
protein

Makes a 9 x 13 sheet cake

Great for a first birthday cake, topped with Cream Cheese Icing!

$1/2$ cup margarine at room temperature
3 eggs
$3/4$ cup unsweetened pineapple juice
1 cup whole wheat flour
$1 1/2$ cups unbleached white flour
$1/3$ cup wheat germ
1 teaspoon baking soda
3 teaspoons low-sodium baking powder
1 teaspoon nutmeg
$1 1/2$ teaspoons cinnamon
$3 1/4$ cups grated carrots
1 cup crushed pineapple, unsweetened
and well drained

Preheat oven to 350°. Cream together the eggs and margarine and then stir in the pineapple juice. Add flours, wheat germ, baking soda, baking powder, and spices. Mix thoroughly. Stir in grated carrots and pineapple. Coat a 9 x 13 baking pan with vegetable cooking spray. Pour in batter and spread to an even layer. Bake until center springs back when touched, about 30–35 minutes. Allow to cool before slicing.

Sugar Ratings For Store-bought Foods

When It Has To Be Quick: Product Evaluations Of Store-bought Foods

- - - - - - - - - - - - - - - - - - - -

As a member of a two-job household, I fully appreciate the need to have prepackaged foods and snacks at my fingertips. There just is not always time to bake or prepare a homemade recipe. As I increasingly found myself tempted to grab a Fig Newton and hand it to my daughter (there's some fruit in it, right?), I began to search for healthful alternatives. I certainly didn't want to be feeding my toddler Honey Nut Cheerios at 36 percent sucrose when I could select regular Cheerios at 3.5 percent sucrose instead. And, too, I did not want her to feel slighted when her pals at day care ate cookies and muffins, but I also recognized that most of the treats commonly served are full of empty calories. Since toddlers eat a limited amount of food everyday anyway, it compounds the problem when they eat a non-nutritive food. The non-nutritive food simply replaces a nutritive food that would have been eaten. Toddlers, unlike adults, can't and don't compensate for their junk food snacks by eating a larger amount of nutritious food "later."

With this in mind, I began to look for healthful alternatives. I found many more than I had ever anticipated! There is a huge array of products out there that are sugar-free and made with nutritious ingredients, from cookies to breakfast cereals. Keep in mind that even with so-called health foods, you must read the ingredient label. Many products use honey, concentrated fructose, molasses, and maple syrup as sweeteners, so buyer beware. Even after I eliminated those, I still ended up with a great variety of foods that were nutritious and sugar-free.

What follows is a listing of many of the products I found, tested, and researched, with a brief evaluation of their quality and appropriateness for toddlers. The specific products in each category are listed in descending order, most preferable to least preferable. I have also included for comparison purposes many sugared foods similar to the unsugared ones, with their sugar content listed. Sugar contents of sugared items are listed by the percentage of total calories in the product attributable to sucrose. So if a cookie had 50 calories, and 25 of these were from sucrose, the percentage listed would be 50 percent. These figures allow you to make informed choices for your family. For obvious reasons, I have not tried to create an all-inclusive list of all products that are on the market. Rather, I have tried to include a cross-section of products that are most readily available in most areas.

Availability

More and more of these healthful products are now available in grocery stores which makes them even more convenient for most people. However, many products are still available only in health food stores and natural food cooperatives. But don't let this stop you from becoming more sugar-free. In our family, we try to limit our forays into health food stores to once per month by buying enough of the few products we need to last our family the entire month. This has worked fairly well, although there have been times when all of the ginger snaps have mysteriously disappeared and an extra trip was necessary.

Note: With nearly all of the sugar-free products, extra care is needed to maintain the freshness of the product. Since most of these products have no additives or preservatives, they tend to dry out faster than you may be accustomed to. Always store them in airtight (and preferably light-impermeable) containers.

Big Differences

Once you glance through these product comparisons you'll see that you can make a tremendous difference in the amount of empty sucrose calories your toddler consumes, simply by reaching for the more appropriate package on the supermarket shelf. I believe most every parent would avoid Apple Jacks cereal at a whopping 54 percent of its calories attributable to sugar when it is just as easy to reach for a cereal with zero percent sucrose. Why buy fruit roll-ups at 40 percent (estimated) calories in sucrose when you can buy other fruit leathers (or better yet make your own using the recipe in this book) with zero percent sucrose?

Calculating Cereal Sugar Content

To make rough calculations of a cereal's sugar content, take the figure which says "Sucrose and other sugars" on the cereal box. Divide the number of grams of "sucrose and other sugars" by 30 to calculate the percentage of sugars in the cereal. A cereal with 3 grams of "sucrose and other sugars" would have 10 percent sugars. However, this number will include the fructose and natural sugars in cereals with dried fruit, so keep that in mind in your calculations.

A Few Words About Vitamins

If your pediatrician considers it important for your child to take a vitamin supplement, choose carefully. Many of the brand name chewable vitamins in particular are up to 50 percent sucrose by weight. Most of the brand name infant vitamin drops contain no sugar, but check the labels— some do contain small amounts of sucrose.

Chewable tablets:		percent of sucrose by weight
Ayerst Labs:	Cluvisol Multivitamins	0.0
Rugby Labs:	Children's Chewables	5.3
Ross Labs:	Vi-Daylin tablets	26.3
Mead-Johnson:	Poly-Vi-Sol tablets	21.0
	Poly-Vi-Flor tablets	44.1
Miles Labs:	Chocks/Flintstones	55.9

Vitamin Drops:		percent of sucrose by weight
Mead-Johnson:	Poly-Vi-Sol	0.0
	Tri-Vi-Sol	0.0
Rugby Labs:	Poly Vitamin Drops	0.0
	Tri-Vitamin Drops	0.0
	Deca-Vite Drops	3.4
Twin Labs:	Infant Care Multivitamin Drops	0.0

There are a number of natural chewable vitamins available in health food stores. Be sure you know what you are looking for, because labels can be misleading, and you will pay a premium price for vitamins of any kind in most health food stores.

Product Evaluations

Toaster pastries

Nature's Warehouse

Pastry Poppers

FLAVOR:	strawberry, apple, cherry, raspberry, peach-apricot, blueberry
CALORIES:	212 per pastry
SWEETENER:	fruit juice
TODDLER RATING:	9
% CALORIES: ATTRIBUTABLE TO SUGAR	0%

These are flavorful and fruity. Some kids prefer them untoasted, right out of the box. They are more crumbly than their sugared counterparts (Poptarts), so it is important to keep them fresh once opened. Each pastry is sealed in an individual foil wrapper. Strawberry and apple flavors are made with whole wheat flour. The other flavors are wheat-free and made with oat and barley flour. No tropical oils. The oil used is canola, a nonhydrogenated vegetable oil. About 56 mg sodium per pastry.

Kellogg's

Poptarts

FLAVOR:	8 unfrosted flavors, 9 frosted flavors
CALORIES:	210 per pastry
SWEETENER:	sucrose
TODDLER RATING:	
% CALORIES: ATTRIBUTABLE TO SUGAR	unfrosted = 27.5% ; frosted = 31% About 250 mg sodium per pastry.

Animal Crackers

Westbrae Natural Foods

Dino Snaps

FLAVOR:	lemon, vanilla, ginger, and oatmeal raisin
CALORIES:	15 per cookie
SWEETENER:	fruit juice
TODDLER RATING:	10
% CALORIES: ATTRIBUTABLE TO SUGAR	0%

These are small cookies with a light flavor that toddlers enjoy. They are shaped like four kinds of dinosaurs. The package has a picture and name listed for each type. Made with whole wheat flour. No tropical oils.

R.W. Frookie

Animal Frackers

FLAVOR:	vanilla
CALORIES:	10 per cookie
SWEETENER:	fruit juice
TODDLER RATING:	8
% CALORIES: ATTRIBUTABLE TO SUGAR	0%

Their light vanilla flavor and animal shapes appeal to most toddlers, but they are not as crunchy as they should be. These are packed in a variety of sizes, including small handled boxes which toddlers like to carry. Made with whole wheat and unbleached wheat flour, as well as arrowroot flour, which is easily digestible. No tropical oils.

Barbara's Bakery

Animal Cookies

FLAVOR:	carob, cinnamon, vanilla, chocolate
CALORIES:	18 per cookie
SWEETENER:	fruit juice
TODDLER RATING:	8
% CALORIES: ATTRIBUTABLE TO SUGAR	0%

A somewhat heavier flavor than traditional animal crackers. Too soft a texture - needs more crunch. These are also packed in a variety of package sizes, including small handled boxes. Made with whole wheat flour. No tropical oils. Made with canola oil.

Nabisco

Barnum's Animal Crackers

FLAVOR:	vanilla
CALORIES:	65 per cookie
SWEETENER:	
TODDLER RATING:	
% CALORIES: ATTRIBUTABLE TO SUGAR	24%

Breakfast Cereal
O's Cereals

New Morning

Oatios, Fruit-E-O's

FLAVOR:	oat, fruit
CALORIES:	110 per 1 oz. serving
SWEETENER:	fruit juice
TODDLER RATING:	9
% CALORIES: ATTRIBUTABLE TO SUGAR	0%

These are crunchy and flavorful. 2.4 gm dietary fiber per 1 oz. serving. No fat or sodium. Made with whole oat flour, oat bran, and brown rice flour. The Fruit-E-O's have a mild but somewhat artificial fruit flavoring (cherry, orange, and lemon).

U.S. Mills/Erewhon

Super O's

FLAVOR:	oat
CALORIES:	110 per 1 oz. serving
SWEETENER:	fruit juice
TODDLER RATING:	9
% CALORIES: ATTRIBUTABLE TO SUGAR	0%

The O's are somewhat large for most toddlers, but they have good crunch and flavor. 4 gm dietary fiber and 5 mg sodium per 1 oz. serving. Very low in fat. Made with oat bran, brown rice flour, corn flour, and whole oat flour.

Barbara's Bakery

Breakfast O's

FLAVOR:	oat
CALORIES:	120 per 1 oz. serving
SWEETENER:	fruit juice
TODDLER RATING:	8
% CALORIES: ATTRIBUTABLE TO SUGAR	0%

These lack the crunch they need, but have good flavor. Very low in fat and now available in many supermarkets. Somewhat higher in sodium than other sugar-free cereals—161 mg sodium per serving. Made with whole oat flour, brown rice flour, and oat bran.

Health Valley

Healthy O's

FLAVOR:	oat
CALORIES:	90 per ¾ cup
SWEETENER:	fruit juice
TODDLER RATING:	7
% CALORIES: ATTRIBUTABLE TO SUGAR	0%

These lack the crunchiness they need to be a mainstay in a toddler's cereal menu, but they have good flavor and stay fresh well. 3.4 gm dietary fiber and 1 mg sodium in each ¾ cup serving. Very little fat.

General Mills

Cheerios

FLAVOR:	oat
CALORIES:	110 per 1 oz. serving
SWEETENER:	sucrose
TODDLER RATING:	9 - 10
% CALORIES: ATTRIBUTABLE TO SUGAR	3.5%

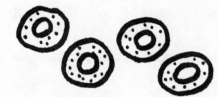

These are very low in sugar and contain 2 gm dietary fiber per 1 oz. serving. They are a not-too-bad alternative if you can not find any sugar-free cereals. 2 gm fat and 290 mg sodium per serving. Don't confuse these with Honey Nut Cheerios, with 36% of its calories attributable to sucrose!

Rice Crisps

New Morning

Crispy Brown Rice with Amaranth

FLAVOR:	brown rice
CALORIES:	110 per 1 oz serving
SWEETENER:	grain malt
TODDLER RATING:	9
% CALORIES: ATTRIBUTABLE TO SUGAR	0%

A crispy, flavorful cereal high in protein due to the addition of amaranth, a nutritious grain. 2 gm dietary fiber per oz. No sodium and low fat (1 gm per oz.). Now available in many supermarkets.

U.S. Mills/Erewhon

Low Sodium Crispy Brown Rice Cereal

FLAVOR:	brown rice
CALORIES:	110 per 1 oz. serving
SWEETENER:	barley malt
TODDLER RATING:	9
% CALORIES: ATTRIBUTABLE TO SUGAR	0%

Also crispy and flavorful. Made with brown rice and barley malt.

Barbara's Bakery

Brown Rice Crisps

FLAVOR:	brown rice
CALORIES:	120 per 1.1 oz. serving
SWEETENER:	fruit juice
TODDLER RATING:	9
% CALORIES: ATTRIBUTABLE TO SUGAR	0%

A slightly milder flavor, but still well-liked by toddlers. Made without any barley malt (a grain derivative which has been slightly refined), these are a more natural choice, but are much higher in sodium (300 mg per serving).

Kellogg's

Rice Krispies

FLAVOR:	white rice
CALORIES:	110 per 1 oz. serving
SWEETENER:	sucrose
TODDLER RATING:	9
% CALORIES: ATTRIBUTABLE TO SUGAR	11%

Toddlers actually seem to prefer the brown rice cereals, which have more flavor despite the lack of sucrose. Low in fiber, with 290 mg sodium per serving, these are a less healthful choice than the brown rice choices overall, which are whole-grained.

Puffed Corn and Rice Cereals

Health Valley

Fruit Lites

FLAVOR:	corn, rice, wheat
CALORIES:	50 per ½ oz. serving
SWEETENER:	fruit juice
TODDLER RATING:	10
% CALORIES: ATTRIBUTABLE TO SUGAR	0%

Toddlers love the lightly sweetened flavors of these puffed grain cereals. They look much like their sugared counterparts but are much more nutritious. No fat and very low sodium (2 mg per ½ cup). Each serving has .32 gm dietary fiber.

Arrowhead Mills

Puffed Corn

FLAVOR:	corn, rice, millet
CALORIES:	50 per $\frac{1}{2}$ oz. serving
SWEETENER:	none
TODDLER RATING:	8
% CALORIES: ATTRIBUTABLE TO SUGAR	0%

Many toddlers find this as tasty as the Fruit Lites, but it gets soggy very quickly. However, it costs about half as much as its counterparts, making it appealing to parents. No fat and low sodium (1.4 mg per $\frac{1}{2}$ oz.). 3% dietary fiber by weight.

Kellogg's

Sugar Corn Pops

FLAVOR:	corn
CALORIES:	110 per cup
SWEETENER:	sucrose
TODDLER RATING:	
% CALORIES: ATTRIBUTABLE TO SUGAR	47%

With an extremely high sucrose content, this is worth avoiding.

Corn Flakes

New Morning

Corn Flakes

FLAVOR:	corn
CALORIES:	110 per 1.1 oz.
SWEETENER:	fruit juice
TODDLER RATING:	7
% CALORIES: ATTRIBUTABLE TO SUGAR	0%

Toddlers don't seem to like the soggy texture of corn flakes in general, but liked these as well as the sugared ones. Low in sodium. Made with corn meal and corn bran, and 3.9 gm fiber per 1.1 oz. serving. This is the healthiest and tastiest choice for corn flakes.

Barbara's Bakery

Corn Flakes

FLAVOR:	corn
CALORIES:	110 per oz.
SWEETENER:	fruit juice
TODDLER RATING:	7
% CALORIES: ATTRIBUTABLE TO SUGAR	0%

See above for corn flakes in general. Nearly as high in sodium (310 mg per serving) as the sugared alternative, but higher in dietary fiber.

Kellogg's
Corn Flakes

FLAVOR:	corn
CALORIES:	110 per 1 cup serving
SWEETENER:	sucrose
TODDLER RATING:	7
% CALORIES: ATTRIBUTABLE TO SUGAR	11%

Again, the soggy texture was a negative. Only 1 gm fiber per 1 oz. serving. With 320 mg sodium, the Kellogg's variety stacks up closely to Barbara's, but it lacks the fiber.

Kellogg's
Frosted Flakes

FLAVOR:	sugar-coated corn
CALORIES:	110 per 1 oz. serving
SWEETENER:	sucrose
TODDLER RATING:	
% CALORIES: ATTRIBUTABLE TO SUGAR	37%

Frosted Flakes' high sucrose content makes it a cereal to avoid.

**In Brief:
Other Cereals For Comparison**

Post
*Grape Nuts & Grape Nut-
Flakes*
0%

Quaker
Puffed Wheat and Rice
0%

General Mills
Kix
7%

Ralston
Corn Chex
7.5%

Quaker
Life
19%

General Mills
Honey Nut Cheerios
36%
Don't confuse these
with the plain Cheerios!

Post
Alpha-Bits
40%

Quaker
Cap'n Crunch
40%

Kellogg's
Fruit Loops
47%

Kellogg's
Apple Jacks
54%

Fruit Leather

	Nature's Choice/Barbara's Bakery
	Real Fruit Bars
FLAVOR:	apricot, cherry, grape, apple, raspberry
CALORIES:	50 per bar
SWEETENER:	fruit
TODDLER RATING:	9 - 10
% CALORIES: ATTRIBUTABLE TO SUGAR	0%

These are much easier to chew than other leathers due to the
addition of pectin and guar gum. Toddlers prefer the texture
and generally love to eat these. They also fulfill about 1/2 a fruit
serving. All natural with no additives.

Stretch Island

Fruit Leather/Fruit Ripples

FLAVOR:	many flavors
CALORIES:	45 for 1 bar of fruit leather, 50 for 1 bar of fruit ripples
SWEETENER:	fruit
TODDLER RATING:	8
% CALORIES: ATTRIBUTABLE TO SUGAR	0%

These are somewhat difficult to chew and are thus not recommended for very young children. They have good, natural flavor and one fulfills about $^1/_2$ a fruit serving for a toddler. The pina colada flavor has a small amount of honey added.

Betty Crocker/General Mills

Fruit Roll-Ups

FLAVOR:	cherry, fruit punch, grape, raspberry, strawberry, watermelon
CALORIES:	50 per bar
SWEETENER:	sucrose
TODDLER RATING:	
% CALORIES: ATTRIBUTABLE TO SUGAR	40% (estimated)

These are much more a candy than a fruit snack and contain only minimal amounts of fruit. They contain corn syrup, sugar, and confectioner's glaze.

Peanut Butter

Health Valley
Creamy or Chunky Peanut Butter

U.S. Mills
Creamy or Chunky Salt-Free Peanut Butter

Peter Pan/Beatrice
Creamy Peter Pan Salt-Free Peanut Butter

All of these are sodium-free and sugar-free. They all taste very good and are good alternatives to peanut butters with additives and sugars. However, natural peanut butters are preferable to name-brand, highly processed peanut butters. Manufacturers of processed peanut butters usually partly hydrogenate the oil in order to keep it from separating.

	Skippy
	Creamy Peanut Butter
FLAVOR:	
CALORIES:	190 calories for 2 tbsp.
SWEETENER:	sucrose
TODDLER RATING:	
% CALORIES: ATTRIBUTABLE TO SUGAR	4%

With a much higher sodium content (about 190 mg per 2 tbsp.) than natural peanut butters that have only trace amounts, the average store-bought peanut butter is much less healthy for your toddler.

Apple Butter

Shiloh Farms

Apple Butter

FLAVOR:	apple
CALORIES:	unavailable but estimated as minimal
SWEETENER:	none
TODDLER RATING:	9
% CALORIES: ATTRIBUTABLE TO SUGAR	0%

Toddlers love the apple-cinnamon flavor of apple butter. This non-sugared alternative has been almost unanimously popular. Available in many health food stores and also through mail order.

New Morning

Apple Butter

FLAVOR:	apple
CALORIES:	unavailable but estimated as minimal
SWEETENER:	none
TODDLER RATING:	9
% CALORIES: ATTRIBUTABLE TO SUGAR	0%

Very similar to Shiloh Farms.

Smucker's

Spiced Apple Butter

FLAVOR:	apple-spice
CALORIES:	25 for 2 tsp.
SWEETENER:	sucrose
TODDLER RATING:	
% CALORIES: ATTRIBUTABLE TO SUGAR	80%

Although tasty, its extremely high sugar content makes this and other sugared apple butters a less attractive product than its natural counterparts.

Fruit Juices

Bowman

Daisey Fresh Juices

FLAVOR:	tropical fruit, pineapple-coconut, apple-papaya, and others
CALORIES:	unavailable
SWEETENER:	none
TODDLER RATING:	10
% CALORIES: ATTRIBUTABLE TO SUGAR	0%

These 100% pure juices are a favorite of nearly all toddlers. The apple-strawberry seems to be the most popular, because it is not quite as sweet as the others.

McCain

McCain Junior Juice

FLAVOR:	apple, apple-cherry, mixed fruit
CALORIES:	75 per 4.2 oz.
SWEETENER:	none
TODDLER RATING:	10
% CALORIES: ATTRIBUTABLE TO SUGAR	0%

Small 4.2 oz. boxes of juice with straws. The perfect size for toddlers who never seem to finish the larger juice boxes. 100% pure.

Knudsen & Sons, Inc.

R.W. Knudsen Juices

FLAVOR:	apple-raspberry, papaya nectar, cherry cider, and others
CALORIES:	unavailable
SWEETENER:	none
TODDLER RATING:	9
% CALORIES: ATTRIBUTABLE TO SUGAR	0%

Knudsen's innovative recombination of flavors has yielded a group of very tasty juices which everyone seems to like (except the very veggie flavor, which toddlers aren't crazy about). 100% pure juices.

S. Martinelli & Co.

Pure Apple Juice and Sparkling Cider

FLAVOR:	apple
CALORIES:	unavailable
SWEETENER:	none
TODDLER RATING:	9
% CALORIES: ATTRIBUTABLE TO SUGAR	0%

Martinelli offers pure apple juice in small individual glass bottles, to help maintain freshness. Cheaper than baby juices and nice for those times when a large bottle might spoil, once opened.

Nestle Foods Corp.

Juicy Juice

FLAVOR:	cherry, tropical, grape
CALORIES:	150 per 8.45 oz. box
SWEETENER:	none
TODDLER RATING:	9
% CALORIES: ATTRIBUTABLE TO SUGAR	0%

Readily available 100% juices, available in 3-packs of individual boxes.

ATF, Inc.
After The Fall Juices

FLAVOR:	pear, apple, Oregonberry blend, apple-apricot, apple-strawberry
CALORIES:	unavailable
SWEETENER:	none
TODDLER RATING:	8
% CALORIES: ATTRIBUTABLE TO SUGAR	0%

Also 100% pure, these seem to be too strongly flavored for many toddlers. Several flavors are now available in individual juice boxes.

Ocean Spray
Cranberry Juice Cocktail

FLAVOR:	cranberry
CALORIES:	165 per cup
SWEETENER:	sucrose
TODDLER RATING:	
% CALORIES: ATTRIBUTABLE TO SUGAR	50%

With so many sugar-free choices readily available, why choose this or any of the following?

Hi-C

Flavored soft drinks

FLAVOR:	grape, lemonade, orange, punch
CALORIES:	80 per 6 oz.
SWEETENER:	sucrose
TODDLER RATING:	
% CALORIES: ATTRIBUTABLE TO SUGAR	97%

Almost all of its calories attributable to sugar!

Sundor Brands, Inc.

Hawaiian Punch

FLAVOR:	fruit punch
CALORIES:	90 per 6 oz.
SWEETENER:	sucrose
TODDLER RATING:	
% CALORIES: ATTRIBUTABLE TO SUGAR	90%(estimated)

Carnation

Instant Breakfast

FLAVOR:	vanilla, chocolate, chocolate malt, coffee, eggnog, strawberry
CALORIES:	130 per pouch
SWEETENER:	sucrose
TODDLER RATING:	
% CALORIES: ATTRIBUTABLE TO SUGAR	60%

Kraft General Foods, Inc.

Kool-Aid Soft Drink Mix

FLAVOR:	many flavors
CALORIES:	100 per 8 oz.
SWEETENER:	sucrose
TODDLER RATING:	
% CALORIES: ATTRIBUTABLE TO SUGAR	98%

Kraft General Foods, Inc.

Tang

FLAVOR:	orange
CALORIES:	60 per 4 oz.
SWEETENER:	sucrose
TODDLER RATING:	
% CALORIES: ATTRIBUTABLE TO SUGAR	96%

Teething Biscuits

Healthy Times

All-Natural Biscuits For Teethers

FLAVOR:	vanilla
CALORIES:	49 per biscuit
SWEETENER:	unsulphured molasses (in minimal amounts)
TODDLER RATING:	9
% CALORIES: ATTRIBUTABLE TO SUGAR	unavailable

I have included these in spite of their slight molasses sweetener, because there are so few convenient alternatives available. Light flavor and appropriately firm texture. Made with whole wheat flour, raw wheat germ, unsulphured molasses, whey, water, safflower oil, and vanilla extract.

Nabisco

Zwieback Teething Toast

FLAVOR:	plain
CALORIES:	60 per piece
SWEETENER:	beet and cane sugar
TODDLER RATING:	
% CALORIES: ATTRIBUTABLE TO SUGAR	unavailable

Unfortunately, these popular toasts are full of refined sugar. Although the exact percent is unavailable, it is estimated to be very high. Either homemade or the Healthy Times brand are good alternatives. See the recipe for Teething Stix in chapter 6. No tropical oils.

Arrowroot Cookies

Healthy Times

Arrowroot Cookies for Toddlers

FLAVOR:	vanilla, maple
CALORIES:	
SWEETENER:	low acid grape juice, unsulphured molasses (in minimal amounts)
TODDLER RATING:	9
% CALORIES: ATTRIBUTABLE TO SUGAR	unavailable

I have included these in spite of their slight molasses sweetener, because there are so few arrowroot flour alternatives. Good for toddlers and easily digestible, arrowroot flour is a mildly-flavored grain appropriate for even very young toddlers. No tropical oils.

Nabisco

National Arrowroot Biscuits

FLAVOR:	vanilla
CALORIES:	21 per biscuit
SWEETENER:	sucrose
TODDLER RATING:	9
% CALORIES: ATTRIBUTABLE TO SUGAR	19%

Made with refined flours and sugars, this brand of arrowroot cookie is a less healthful alternative than even the unsulphured molasses-sweetened cookies that are made with whole wheat flours and fruit juice.

Fig Cookies/Bars

R.W. Frookie Fruitins

FLAVOR:	fig, apple
CALORIES:	60 per cookie
SWEETENER:	fruit juice, fruit
TODDLER RATING:	10
% CALORIES: ATTRIBUTABLE TO SUGAR	0%

These are top of the line! Soft and chewy, but lightly textured. Absolutely delicious. Made with whole wheat flour, oat flour, and oat bran. 25 mg sodium and 1 gm fat (polyunsaturated) per cookie.

Health Valley

Fruit Bakes

FLAVOR:	apple, date, raisin
CALORIES:	100 per bar
SWEETENER:	fruit juice, fruit
TODDLER RATING:	7
% CALORIES: ATTRIBUTABLE TO SUGAR	0%

Large and heavy, these seem too grainy for toddlers. Made with whole wheat flour. Low in sodium (20-25 mg per bar) and fat. No tropical oils.

Nature's Warehouse

Fig Bars

FLAVOR:	whole wheat fig, wheat-free fig, apple cinnamon fig, raspberry fig
CALORIES:	98 per bar
SWEETENER:	fruit juice, fruit
TODDLER RATING:	7
% CALORIES: ATTRIBUTABLE TO SUGAR	0%

Well-sized for children, but with a flavor that is too heavy and grainy-tasting. Low in fat. Made with whole wheat or barley flour, and canola oil.

J&J Snack Foods Corp.

Pride O' The Farm Fruit Prides

FLAVOR:	raisin, date, apple
CALORIES:	75 per bar
SWEETENER:	fruit juices, fruit
TODDLER RATING:	7
% CALORIES: ATTRIBUTABLE TO SUGAR	0%

These are also fairly large and heavy. Their flavor varieties are more distinct, but are too grainy for most kids. These are made with dates rather than figs, but are very similar to fig bars. Made with whole wheat flour, oat bran, and wheat germ. Low sodium (26 mg per bar) and fat (2.5 gm per bar). They have 1.8 gm dietary fiber per bar.

Nabisco

Fig Newtons

FLAVOR:	fig, apple, raspberry, cinnamon raisin nut
CALORIES:	60 per cookie
SWEETENER:	sucrose, fruit
TODDLER RATING:	
% CALORIES: ATTRIBUTABLE TO SUGAR	51%

Made with refined flours and sugars. 62 mg sodium per cookie.

Soft Cookies

R.W. Frookie

Frookies

FLAVOR:	ginger spice, chocolate chip, oatmeal raisin, oat bran muffin
CALORIES:	45 per cookie
SWEETENER:	fruit juice
TODDLER RATING:	10
% CALORIES: ATTRIBUTABLE TO SUGAR	0%, except chocolate chips

These cookies are soft and lightly flavored. They are perfectly sized for small hands. Delicious! The chocolate chips contain sucanat brand sweetener, made of evaporated fresh cane juice. It contains small amounts of magnesium, phosphorus, chromium, and vitamins A,B, and C. No tropical oils. Made with unbleached wheat flour and oat bran. 40 mg sodium and 2 gm fat per cookie.

Lady J

Original Lady J Cookies

FLAVOR:	orange-pineapple, brown rice, banana, peanut butter, and others
CALORIES:	unavailable
SWEETENER:	fruit juice
TODDLER RATING:	9
% CALORIES: ATTRIBUTABLE TO SUGAR	0%

A nice, light chewy texture and light flavors place these among toddlers' favorite cookies. Made with whole wheat flour and oats. No tropical oils.

Nature's Warehouse

Fruitsweet Cookies

FLAVOR:	oatmeal raisin, peanut butter, carob fudge, coconut, and others
CALORIES:	65 per cookie
SWEETENER:	fruit juice and fruit
TODDLER RATING:	8.5
% CALORIES: ATTRIBUTABLE TO SUGAR	0%

Nearly all flavors of these cookies are well-liked by toddlers. They particularly seem to like the orange and almond butter varieties. Wheat-free varieties include oat bran, almond butter, and brown rice and barley. They also have 3 chocolate chip varieties, with barley malt used to sweeten the chips. Made with canola oil, whole wheat flour, oat flour, and oat bran. Low sodium (25 mg per cookie) and low fat (3-4 gm unsaturated).

J&J Snack Foods Corp.

Pride O' The Farm All Natural Cookies

FLAVOR:	oatmeal raisin, carob chip, peanut butter, and others
CALORIES:	60-65 per cookie
SWEETENER:	fruit, fruit juice
TODDLER RATING:	8.5
% CALORIES: ATTRIBUTABLE TO SUGAR	0%

These are more fruity-flavored and lighter than most. Very moist and just chewy enough for toddlers. Also have wheat free and gluten free varieties. 30-35 mg sodium and 2 gm fat per cookie. No tropical oils.

Barbara's Bakery

Drop Cookies

FLAVOR:	fruit & nut, oatmeal raisin, tropical coconut, and others
CALORIES:	30-60 per cookie
SWEETENER:	fruit juice
TODDLER RATING:	8
% CALORIES: ATTRIBUTABLE TO SUGAR	0%

These are somewhat dry and thin-textured, but many toddlers enjoy them. Made with whole wheat flour and canola oil. No sodium, no tropical oils.

Cathy's Cookies

Cathy's Cookies

FLAVOR:	almond, carob chip, cinnamon raisin, coconut macaroon
CALORIES:	60-70 per cookie
SWEETENER:	fruit juice
TODDLER RATING:	8
% CALORIES: ATTRIBUTABLE TO SUGAR	0%

Fairly flavorful and with a good chewy texture. Flavors are distinct; cookies are well-sized for toddlers.

Pillsbury

Slice 'N Bake

FLAVOR:	chocolate chip, fudge brownie, oatmeal, peanut butter, sugar
CALORIES:	45-55 per cookie
SWEETENER:	sucrose, molasses
TODDLER RATING:	
% CALORIES: ATTRIBUTABLE TO SUGAR	39%

Along with high sucrose content, contains hydrogenated vegetable oils.

Crisp Cookies

J&J Snack Foods

Pride O'The Farm Crisps

FLAVOR:	sesame, carrot, cinnamon, chocolate
CALORIES:	22-25 calories per cookie
SWEETENER:	fruit juice
TODDLER RATING:	9
% CALORIES: ATTRIBUTABLE TO SUGAR	0%

These are well-sized and have a nice full flavor without being overpowering. Great for teethers! Made with whole wheat and soy flours. Low sodium (about 12 mg per cookie) and fat (1 gm per cookie). No tropical oils.

Barbara's Bakery

Deluxe Sandwich Cookies

FLAVOR:	fudge, lemon, and vanilla sandwich cremes
CALORIES:	65 per cookie
SWEETENER:	fruit juice
TODDLER RATING:	5
% CALORIES: ATTRIBUTABLE TO SUGAR	0%

Unfortunately, these look much better than they taste. They are too soft and have a very bland flavor. Few toddlers would eat them. Made with whole wheat flour and canola oil. No tropical oils.

In Brief: Crisp Cookies

Nabisco

Chips Ahoy

FLAVOR:	chocolate chip
CALORIES:	53 per cookie
SWEETENER:	sucrose
TODDLER RATING:	
% CALORIES: ATTRIBUTABLE TO SUGAR	24%

Nabisco

Bakers Bonus Oatmeal Cookies

FLAVOR:	oatmeal
CALORIES:	80 per cookie
SWEETENER:	sucrose
TODDLER RATING:	
% CALORIES: ATTRIBUTABLE TO SUGAR	41%

Nabisco

Honey Maid Graham Crackers

FLAVOR:	plain, honey, cinnamon
CALORIES:	30 per cracker
SWEETENER:	sucrose, honey
TODDLER RATING:	
% CALORIES: ATTRIBUTABLE TO SUGAR	30%

Nabisco

Oreos

FLAVOR:	chocolate cookies with vanilla creme centers
CALORIES:	50 each
SWEETENER:	sucrose
TODDLER RATING:	
% CALORIES: ATTRIBUTABLE TO SUGAR	44%

The cream filling contains lard.

Ginger Snaps

R.W. Frookie

Gingerbread Friends

FLAVOR:	ginger
CALORIES:	25 per cookie
SWEETENER:	fruit juices
TODDLER RATING:	10
% CALORIES: ATTRIBUTABLE TO SUGAR	0%

Frookie does it again! Indistinguishable from their sugared counterparts, these are crispy and delicious. Small cookies shaped like gingerboys and -girls. Made with unbleached wheat flour, whole wheat flour, soybean oil. Low fat (1 gm) and sodium (32 mg). No tropical oils.

Westbrae Natural Foods

Ginger Snaps

FLAVOR:	ginger
CALORIES:	43 per cookie
SWEETENER:	rice syrup, raisin juice
TODDLER RATING:	8+
% CALORIES: ATTRIBUTABLE TO SUGAR	0%

These have a nice crispy texture (great for teethers!) but are too grainy to have overall appeal.

Nabisco

Old Fashioned Ginger Snaps

FLAVOR:	ginger
CALORIES:	30 per cookie
SWEETENER:	unavailable
TODDLER RATING:	
% CALORIES: ATTRIBUTABLE TO SUGAR	51%

Made with refined flour. 46 mg sodium per cookie.

Frozen Juice Bars

Dole

Suntops Frozen Juice Bars

FLAVOR:	fruit punch, lemonade, grape, orange
CALORIES:	40 per bar
SWEETENER:	none
TODDLER RATING:	10
% CALORIES: ATTRIBUTABLE TO SUGAR	0%

Excellent! Just the right sweetness with a full fruity flavor. 5 mg sodium and less than 1 gm fat per bar.

Natural Nectar Corp.

Frozen Juice Bars

FLAVOR:	Tropical Delite, Lemony Lime
CALORIES:	63 per bar
SWEETENER:	fruit juice
TODDLER RATING:	9
% CALORIES: ATTRIBUTABLE TO SUGAR	0%

These frozen treats are a bit tart, but nearly all toddlers gave them the thumbs up. Made with white grape juice and natural flavors. Low in fat and sodium.

Popsicle Industries

Twinfruit Popsicle

FLAVOR:	lemon, lime, orange, cherry, grape
CALORIES:	70 per Popsicle
SWEETENER:	unavailable
TODDLER RATING:	
% CALORIES: ATTRIBUTABLE TO SUGAR	91%

There is no need to buy these when there are healthful alternatives!

Fruit Jams

Polaner

All Fruit Spread

FLAVOR:	10 flavors
CALORIES:	14 per teaspoon
SWEETENER:	fruit
TODDLER RATING:	10
% CALORIES: ATTRIBUTABLE TO SUGAR	0%

These jams are 100% fruit and have a natural full flavor. They are readily available in most grocery stores.

There are several other local and national brands of naturally-sweetened preserves available in your local grocery and health food stores.

Welch's

Jams and Preserves

FLAVOR:	many flavors
CALORIES:	about 16 per teaspoon
SWEETENER:	sucrose
TODDLER RATING:	
% CALORIES: ATTRIBUTABLE TO SUGAR	99% (estimated)

Smucker's

Low Sugar Spreads

FLAVOR:	many flavors
CALORIES:	about 8 per teaspoon
SWEETENER:	unavailable
TODDLER RATING:	
% CALORIES: ATTRIBUTABLE TO SUGAR	88% (estimated)

Although it has half the calories of regular jams and jellies, it retains its high sugar content percentage.

Fruit Toppings (pourable)

R.W. Knudsen

All Fruit Pourable Fruit Toppings

FLAVOR:	blueberry, strawberry, raspberry
CALORIES:	75 per fluid oz.
SWEETENER:	fruit and fruit juice
TODDLER RATING:	10
% CALORIES: ATTRIBUTABLE TO SUGAR	0%

These are excellent! Chunky but still liquid enough to pour easily. Great over waffles or pancakes. Very sweet. Made with chunks of fruit and juice concentrate. No sodium, low fat (1 gm per ounce).

Smucker's

Fruit Syrups

FLAVOR:	blueberry, raspberry, strawberry
CALORIES:	100 per 2 tbsp.
SWEETENER:	sucrose and fruit
TODDLER RATING:	
% CALORIES: ATTRIBUTABLE TO SUGAR	94%

Frozen Waffles

Kellogg's

Nutrigrain Eggo Frozen Waffles

FLAVOR:	whole wheat, raisin & bran, multibran
CALORIES:	130 per waffle
SWEETENER:	fruit juice (multibran) or none (whole wheat and raisin & bran)
TODDLER RATING:	9
% CALORIES: ATTRIBUTABLE TO SUGAR	0%

These are light and airy, with a slight nutty flavor. They keep well and add good, healthful variety to a toddler's meals. Made with whole wheat and wheat bran. The multigrain flavor also contains corn, rice, and oat brans. Relatively high sodium (250 mg per waffle) and relatively low in fat (5 gm per waffle). No tropical oils.

Kellogg's

regular Eggo Waffles

FLAVOR:	plain
CALORIES:	120 per waffle
SWEETENER:	sucrose
TODDLER RATING:	
% CALORIES: ATTRIBUTABLE TO SUGAR	5%

Made with wheat flour. Sodium levels are relatively high at 250 mg per waffle.

Aunt Jemima

Jumbo Waffles

FLAVOR:	buttermilk, original, blueberry
CALORIES:	86 per waffle
SWEETENER:	sucrose
TODDLER RATING:	
% CALORIES: ATTRIBUTABLE TO SUGAR	8 - 10%

Made with wheat flour. High sodium (340 to 465 mg per waffle, depending on the flavor).

Dried Fruit Snacks

Del Monte

Fruit Snacks

FLAVOR:	orchard fruit mix
CALORIES:	70 per .9 oz. (1 packet)
SWEETENER:	fruit
TODDLER RATING:	9
% CALORIES: ATTRIBUTABLE TO SUGAR	0%

Individually packaged dried fruit mix (golden seedless raisins, dried apricots, dried peaches, dried apples, seedless raisins). Most toddlers enjoyed the variety and the flavors. Contains sulphur products to protect color.

Cake Mixes

Fearn Natural Foods

Naturally Flavored Cake Mixes

FLAVOR:	banana, spice, carob, carrot
CALORIES:	unavailable
SWEETENER:	yogurt solids, dry fruit
TODDLER RATING:	9
% CALORIES: ATTRIBUTABLE TO SUGAR	0% (see below)

These mixes call for the addition of $^1/_2$ cup honey as a sweetener, but I substitute apple juice concentrate or white grape juice concentrate directly 1:1, with excellent results. These are well-spiced and flavorful, and maintain good tenderness. Great spread with cream cheese frosting! Made with stone-ground whole wheat flour, soya powder, and dry fruit.

Betty Crocker

Cake Mixes

FLAVOR:	many
CALORIES:	140 per piece
SWEETENER:	sucrose
TODDLER RATING:	
% CALORIES: ATTRIBUTABLE TO SUGAR	64% (estimated)

Made with refined flours and sugars.

Pillsbury

Cake Mixes

FLAVOR:	many
CALORIES:	140 per piece
SWEETENER:	sucrose
TODDLER RATING:	
% CALORIES: ATTRIBUTABLE TO SUGAR	66% (estimated)

Made with refined flours and sugars.

Metric Conversion Tables The charts below compare kitchen measures by weight and by volume to help in converting from the American standard measure to metric measure. To use, look in left hand column for the measure in recipe (for example, cups) and follow along the line to find out what you would like to know (for example, how many milliliters in a cup). Multiply that answer (236) by the number of cups in your recipe—that is, if your recipe calls for 2 cups, you would need 472 milliliters.

U.S. Metric Fluid Volume:

	Fluid Drams	Tea-spoons	Table-spoons	Fluid Ounces	1/4 Cups	Gills 1/2 Cups	Cups	Fluid Pints	Fluid Quarts	Gallons	Milli-liters	Liters
1 Fluid Dram	1	3/4	1/4	1/8 .125	1/16 .0625	.03125	.0156	.0078	.0039	1/1024	3.70	.0037
1 Tea-spoon	1 1/3	1	1/3	1/16	1/12	1/24	1/48	1/96	1/192	1/768	5	.005
1 Table-spoon	4	3	1	1/2	1/4	1/8	1/16	1/32	1/64	1/256	15	.015
1 Fluid Ounce	8	6	2	1	1/2	1/4	1/8	1/16	1/32	1/128	29.56	.030
1/4 Cup	16	12	4	2	1	1/2	1/4	1/8	1/16	1/64	59.125	.059
1 Gill 1/2 Cup	32	24	8	4	2	1	1/2	1/4	1/8	1/32	118.25	.018
1 Cup	64	48	16	8	4	2	1	1/2	1/4	1/16	236	.236
1 Fluid Pint	128	96	32	16	8	4	2	1	1/2	1/8	473	.473
1 Fluid Quart	256	192	64	32	16	8	4	2	1	1/4	946	.946
1 Gallon	1024	768	256	128	64	32	16	8	4	1	3785.4	3.785
1 Milli-liter	.270	.203 or 1/5	.068	.034	.017	.008	.004	.002	.001	.0003	1	.001 or 1/1024
1 Liter	270.5	203.04	67.68	33.814	16.906	8.453	4.227	2.113	1.057	.264	1000	1

U.S. Metric Mass Weight:

	Grains	Drams	Ounces	Pounds	Milligrams	Grams	Kilograms
1 Grain	1	.004	.002	1/7000	64.7	.064	.0006
1 Dram	27.34	1	1/16	1/256	1770	1.77	.002
1 Ounce	437.5	16	1	1/16	2835	28.35	.028
1 Pound	7000	256	16	1	"Lots"	454	.454
1 Milligram	.015	.0006	1/29,000	1/"Lots"	.1	.001	.000001
1 Gram	15.43	.565	.032	.002	1000	1	.001
1 Kilogram	15,430	564.97	.000032	2.2	1,000,000	1000	1

Index

More good books from **Williamson Publishing**

To order additional copies of **Sugar-Free Toddlers**, please enclose $9.95 per copy plus $2.50 shipping and handling. Follow "To Order" instructions on the last page. Thank you.

THE BROWN BAG COOKBOOK:
Nutritious Portable Lunches for Kids and Grown-Ups
by Sara Sloan

Here are more than 1,000 brown bag lunch ideas with 150 recipes for simple, quick, nutritious lunches that kids will love. Breakfast ideas, too! This popular book is now in its sixth printing!

192 pages, 8¼ x 7¼, illustrations,
Quality paperback, $9.95

PARENTS ARE TEACHERS, TOO:
Enriching Your Child's First Six Years
by Claudia Jones

Be the best teacher your child ever has. Jones shares hundreds of ways to help any child learn in playful home situations. Lots on developing reading, writing, math skills. Plenty on creative and critical thinking, too. A book you'll love using!

192 pages, 6 x 9, illustrations,
Quality paperback, $9.95

DOING CHILDREN'S MUSEUMS:
A Guide to 265 Hands–On Museums
by Joanne Cleaver

Turn an ordinary day into a spontaneous "vacation" by
taking a child to some of the 265 participatory children's
museums, discovery rooms, and nature centers covered
in this highly acclaimed, one-of-a-kind book. Filled with
museum specifics to help you pick and plan the perfect place
for the perfect day, Cleaver has created a most valuable
resource for anyone who loves kids!

268 pages, 6 x 9,
Quality paperback, $13.95

KIDS CREATE!
Art & Craft Experiences for 3– to 9–year–olds
by Laurie Carlson

What's the most important experience for children ages 3
to 9? Why to create something by themselves. Carlson
provides over 150 creative experiences ranging from making
dinosaur sculptures to clay cactus gardens, from butterfly
puppets to windsocks. Plenty of help for the parents working
with the kids, too! A delightfully innovative book.

160 pages, 11 x 8½, over 400 illustrations,
Quality paperback, $12.95

THE KIDS' NATURE BOOK:
365 Indoor/Outdoor Activities and Experiences
by Susan Milord

Winner of the Parents' Choice Gold Award for learning and
doing books, *The Kids' Nature Book* is loved by
children, grandparents, and friends alike. Simple projects
and activities emphasize fun while quietly reinforcing
the wonder of the world we all share. Packed with facts
and fun!

160 pages, 12 x 9, 425 illustrations
Quality paperback, $12.95

Easy–to–Make
TEDDY BEARS AND ALL THE TRIMMINGS
by Jodie Davis

Now you can make the most lovable, huggable, plain or
fancy teddy bears imaginable, for a fraction of store-bought
costs. Step-by-step instructions and easy patterns drawn to
actual size for large, soft-bodied bears, quilted bears, and
even jointed bears. Plus patterns for clothes, accessories—
even teddy bear furniture!

192 pages, 8½ x 11, illustrations and patterns,
Quality paperback $13.95

MORE PARENTS ARE TEACHERS, TOO:
Encouraging Your 6– to 12–Year–Old
by Claudia Jones

Help your children be the best they can be! When parents
are involved, kids do better. When kids do better, they feel
better, too. Here's a wonderfully creative book of ideas,
activities, teaching methods, and more to help you help your
children over the rough spots and share in their growing joy
in achieving. Plenty on reading, writing, math, problem-
solving, creative thinking. Everything for parents who want
to help but not push their children.

226 pages, 6 x 9, illustrations,
Quality paperback, $10.95

THE HOMEWORK SOLUTION
by Linda Agler Sonna

Put homework responsibilities where they belong—in the
student's lap! Here it is! The simple remedy for the millions
of parents who are tired of waging the never–ending nightly
battle over kids' homework. Dr. Sonna's "One Step Solution"
will relieve parents, kids and their siblings of the ongoing
problem within a single month.

192 pages, 6 x 9,
Quality paperback, $10.95

GOLDE'S HOMEMADE COOKIES
by Golde Soloway

Over 50,000 copies of this marvelous cookbook have been sold. Now it's in its second edition with 135 of the most delicious cookie recipes imaginable. *Publishers Weekly* says, "Cookies are her chosen realm and how sweet a world it is to visit." You're sure to agree!

162 pages, 8¼ x 7¼, illustrations
Quality paperback, $8.95

ADVENTURES IN ART
Art & Craft Experiences for 7– to 14–year–olds
by Susan Milord

Imagine an art book that encourages children to explore, to experience, to touch and to see, to learn and to create...imagine a true adventure in art. Here's a book that teaches artisan's skills without stifling creativity. Covers making handmade papers, puppets, masks, paper seascapes, seed art, tin can lantern, berry ink, still life, silk screen, batiking, carving, and so much more. Perfect for the older child. Let the adventure begin!

160 pages 11 x 8½, 500 illustrations
Quality paperback, $12.95

To Order:
At your bookstore or order directly from Williamson Publishing. We accept Visa and MasterCard (please include number and expiration date), or send check to:

Williamson Publishing Company
Church Hill Road, P.O. Box 185
Charlotte, Vermont 05445

Toll-free phone orders with credit cards:
1–800–234–8791

Please add $2.50 for postage and handling. Satisfaction is guaranteed or full refund without questions or quibbles.